AF592849

NE/SW MAIN LINE ALBUM

NE/SW MAIN LINE ALBUM

John Chalcraft

LONDON

IAN ALLAN LTD

First published 1982

ISBN 0 7110 1172 9

Published by Ian Allan Ltd, Shepperton, Surrey, and printed by Ian Allan Printing Ltd at their works at Coomblands in Runnymede, England.

Front cover: A 'Peak' class locomotive powers a NE/SW train out of Bristol. *John Chalcraft*

Back cover, top: With the locomotive taking it easy it is still possible to see the far end of the ¾-mile long Wickwar tunnel as No 47.079 *G. J. Churchward* emerges from the gloom at the head of the 08.15 Plymouth-Leeds on 4 October 1980.
John Chalcraft

Back cover, bottom: The new order on heavy freight working on the lines of the former Midland Railway are the Doncaster built representatives of Class 56. On 19 June 1980 one of the later members of the class No 56.066 passes Walton upon Trent with a Coalville-Rugeley loaded mgr train. *John Vaughan*

Title page: In wintry conditions on 1 January 1979 the first Inter-City express to pass through Sheffield Brightside station in 1979 headed by a Class 45 whips up the newly fallen snow. *T. Dodgson*

Contents

Introduction

My first recollection of any form of traffic on the North-East/South-West route was that of watching the Paignton-Leeds 'Devonian' leave Bristol Temple Meads in the capable hands of a pair of Stanier 4-6-0s, the normal combination being that of a 'Black Five' and a 'Jubilee'. These locomotives normally took over the working from the Western Region 'Castle' that had worked the train from the south-west. During the mid-1950s the majority of SW/NE trains changed motive power at Temple Meads, the old barriers and rivalry between the Regions still existing despite the passage of nine years since the nationalisation of the various railway systems. Very little changed until the early 1960s when the first diesel-electric 'Peaks' infiltrated the area from the north, however the Western Region's policy of adopting hydraulic transmission for its locomotives meant that many trains still changed power at Bristol and this mode of operation persisted until 1975.

1975 saw the closure of the old Midland station at Gloucester Eastgate and its associated trackwork, necessitating locomotive changes or run round at the rationalised Gloucester Central for trains calling at the city, this rationalisation meant that many of the loco change operations were moved north and trains which changed power provided some of the final regular passenger workings for the doomed 'non-standard' Western Region hydraulics.

Further north the infamous Lickey Incline still provides a difficult obstacle to northbound traffic, but, the modern diesel-electrics with a fast approach to the climb normally breast the summit at 20-30mph, however freight traffic on the route still necessitates the retention of banking locomotives at Bromsgrove although their use is somewhat erratic. Having surmounted the Lickey locomotives face a comparatively easy few miles into Birmingham which is justifiably called the 'hub of the Inter-City network' being a major interchange point for passenger routes and diesel-electric and AC electric traction.

From Birmingham trains face an easy task as they head north across the flood plain of the River Trent through Burton to reach Derby, one time centre of the Midland Railway, beyond Derby the route skirts the eastern flanks of the Pennines before reaching Sheffield, until the late 1970s considerable tonnages of steel traffic originated from this city, but the recession of 1979/80 has severely affected both production and traffic. Beyond Sheffield trains diverge to take routes to York or Leeds through the Yorkshire Coalfield passing the sites of old motive power depots (Royston, Normanton and Leeds Holbeck) which were amongst the last in the country to operate the steam locomotive. By comparison the thriving tourist industry at York owes much to the recently established National Railway Museum which is now the operating base for a large number of the steam locomotives now used on railtours in the area.

The production of this book presented something of a challenge, as a theme it has been the intention to depict the route as probably the most important rail route in the country (with the exception of the prime routes to and from London, although even these do not handle such a wide range of traffic). It has also been the intention to make the illustrations and captions as informative as possible, although it has proved difficult to obtain early 1970s material, the majority of photographers having apparently hung up their cameras from the end of steam to the mid-1970s leaving vast gaps in the unused material readily available, others may argue that the NE/SW route really starts and finishes at Plymouth (or Penzance?) and Newcastle, but these extremities already receive extensive coverage and for this reason are omitted. However, with these omissions in mind it is hoped that the end product will be of some interest and use to the railway enthusiast as he travels the line. Sincere thanks are due to photographer colleagues and British Rail personnel without whose help I would have been unable to complete the project.

John Chalcraft
May 1981

Cardiff-Gloucester

The entry and exit from Cardiff can hardly be described as interesting except possibly to the student of industrial architecture, but, this area and the valleys to the north of the city are responsible for a large percentage of the rail traffic (predominantly freight that originates from South Wales). Staple power for the majority of South Wales traffic in the area is provided by Canton's large allocation of Classes 37 and 47 although the majority of passenger workings are in the hands of eth fitted '45s' and '47s' not based within the area.

From Cardiff the line travels east along the coastal plain to reach Newport, passing Ebbw Junction depot on the left, the depot provides power for the local valley lines, trip freight working and traffic originating from the docks although it has no main line allocation of its own, usual power being in the form of Canton's '37s', '47s' and '56s'. There is considerable local traffic to and from the giant BSC steelworks at Llanwern which is built on the coastal plain to the east of the town, after passing Llanwern the extensive marshalling yards at Severn Tunnel Junction are soon reached, the majority of wagonload freight traffic within the area is sorted at Severn Tunnel Junction before further distribution throughout the country or South Wales and a wide range of visiting motive power can be seen. East of Severn Tunnel Junction the main Western Region route to London diverges to drop into the Severn Tunnel while the NE/SW route follows the western bank of the Bristol Channel to pass beneath the Severn Bridge before reaching Chepstow where the line crosses the River Wye, at this point a glance back provides an excellent view of Chepstow castle before the line plunges into a rock cutting, re-emerging to run along the Severn Estuary past Lydney and Newnham before turning away from the river although crossing over same just before entering Gloucester.

Left: The low evening sun on October 1980 highlights eth Class 47 No 47.464 as it leads the Mk 2 stock for the 17.45 Cardiff-Sheffield out of Canton's carriage sidings and into Cardiff Central station. *John Chalcraft*

Right: The west end of Cardiff Central station on 2 October 1980 as HST car No 43.121 noses out of the station, one of the non-boilered variations of Class 47 No 47.335 takes the through road with a train of 100tonne oil tanks from Milford Haven. *John Chalcraft*

Below: A short distance to the east of Cardiff Central a short branch line diverges from the main route giving access to Cardiff Docks and the GKN works, a considerable amount of traffic between Cardiff and Scunthorpe originates from the steelworks. On 2 October 1980 Class 37 No 37.185 ambles off of the branch to join the main line at the head of 16.55 Cardiff Tidal Sidings to Llanwern trip freight working. *John Chalcraft*

Above: Pengam Sidings lie some two miles east of Cardiff Central and provide a base for Freightliner movements originating from Cardiff. On 2 October 1980 having arrived with the Swansea (Danygraig) portion of its train No 56.044 shunts and marshalls stock for the depot before coupling the stock to that already in the holding sidings, after the shunting operation the locomotive will run round the stock before departing for Stratford Freightliner terminal. *John Chalcraft*

Left: A somewhat older example of rail operations in the Cardiff area, both the locomotive and sidings have now passed into oblivion, having completed shunting operations of tank wagons at Marshfield, 'Hymek' (later Class 35) No D7080 in green livery prepares to propel its train back to Cardiff, the date is 18 August 1968. *P. J. Fowler*

Above: Having passed Newport's Ebbw junction depot No 37.244 ambles past Alexandra Dock junction with an unfitted Coke train bound for BSC Llanwern, at the same time a train of empty mgr wagons from Didcot power station is led into the docks area by No 56.046 on 30 September 1980.
John Chalcraft

Right: Eth fitted 'Peak' No 45.115 slows for its Newport stop on 6 June 1979 as it passes Gaer junction and approaches the Newport tunnels at the head of the 17.45 Cardiff-Sheffield, the diverging line gives access to the valley branches to Bedwas, Oakdale, Ebbw Vale and Rose Heyworth. *John Chalcraft*

Left: Shortly before the demise of the 'Blue Pullman' units built by Metro-Cammell, one of the sets (in the two tone Pullman livery), glides into Newport High Street with the up 'South Wales Pullman' on 25 April 1973. In the background a pair of Class 25s Nos 25.155 and 25.170 amble through the station with empty iron ore hoppers, despite their low power these locos spent a period of several years during the mid-1970s based at Canton for duties of this nature.
J. H. Cooper-Smith

Below: Staple motive power for the majority of freight workings in South Wales is now the 1,750hp English Electric Class 37. No 37.239 draws a lengthy train of loaded coal hoppers out of the tunnel and across the track layout to the west of High Street station, Newport to take the through road as it heads for Llanwern on 25 April 1980. *John Chalcraft*

ight: During 1979 Canton depot had everal Class 56s allocated primarily to llow double heading on the Port ablot-Llanwern iron ore trains, initially hey were successful, but it later ecame apparent that all was not well nd Class 37s, triple headed, once again esumed some duties. Nos 37.294, 7.154 and 37.308 head west over the Jsk Bridge into Newport High Street on 5 April 1980. *John Chalcraft*

entre right: Class 37s in their normal uise, as No 37.124 on a westbound rain of vanfits on 20 June 1979, meets a ister member of the class on astbound coal empties as they cross he Usk Bridge to the east of Newport ligh Street station. *raham Scott-Lowe*

ottom right: On a miserably dull April day one of Crewe Depot's boilered Class 25s No 25.055 ambles off of the North and West route onto the main line at Maindee West junction and approaches Newport High Street station with the 12.25 Crewe-Cardiff on 20 April 1980. The reign of the Class 25s has now ended with Class 33s taking over the majority of duties. *John Chalcraft*

Above: Severn Tunnel Junction is a major sorting point for non-block and freight trains to or from South Wales and with the exception of Classes 26 and 27 of the Scottish Region the majority of locomotive classes can be seen in the area. On 16 May 1980 two of Toton's Class 20s, Nos 20.143 and 20.187 ease an unfitted coal train out of the yards past the compact motive power depot. *John Chalcraft*

Left: Class 37, No 37.185 comes to a stand on 20 April 1980 for crew change purposes on one of the roads behind the platforms of Severn Tunnel Junction station, as can be seen the station has been relegated to the status of a halt with the 'bus shelters' common to such installations. The buildings of the old steam depot can be seen in the background behind the first lamp-post. *John Chalcraft*

Above: After several weeks in the lines of stored locomotives outside Swindon Works, Class 46 No 46.028 received a reprieve, it was photographed from the Severn Bridge as it rounded the curve to the west of Chepstow at the head of the 08.32 Manchester Piccadilly-Swansea on 29 November 1980. *John Chalcraft*

Right: On a fine spring morning in April 1980 the passengers waiting at Chepstow watch as No 45.130 accelerates the 10.20 Birmingham-Cardiff away from the speed restricted Wye Bridge and through the station, the passengers will board the following 11.30 Gloucester-Newport stopping service. *Brian Morrison*

Left: No 31.299 ambles through the remains of the Chepstow up platform o 30 May 1980 with a Severn Tunnel Junction-Bescot mixed freight, the olde buildings on the down platform have been replaced by the familiar small stone constructed (vandal proof?) shelter. *John Chalcraft*

Below: On 13 May 1976, the 15.25 Cardiff-Paddington (via Gloucester) service is led across the Wye Bridge as it leaves Chepstow behind 'Western' Class 52 diesel-hydraulic No D1033 *Western Trooper,* sadly, the locomotive and sister class members were eliminated from operating stock during the following nine months. *G. Scott-Lowe*

Above: A small crowd of passengers emerge from the shelter of the Lydney up platform 'bus stop' to join a somewhat shortened Swindon built Cross-Country unit on 8 November 1980. The bracket between the windows indicates that the unit has at some stage been fitted to carry a headlight for Central Wales line duties.
John Chalcraft

Right: The main line from Gloucester to Chepstow receives very little attention from railway photographers although it offers considerable potential particularly where the railway runs alongside the Severn Estuary, on 3 August 1979 eth fitted 'Peak' No 45.130 skirts the estuary as it heads for South Wales at the head of the 10.08 Newcastle-Cardiff.
Roger Kaye

Top: Approximately 1½ miles to the west of Gloucester station lies Over junction, the junction provides access to the small yard which still exists in Gloucester Docks, a regular freight service still exists between the docks and Gloucester Yard, on 30 May 1980 after the passage of the 08.32 Manchester-Swansea and the following stopping service No 08.849 has reversed its train out of the branch and crossed over to the up main line before proceeding to Gloucester Yard. *John Chalcraft*

Above: The Medieval splendour of Gloucester Cathedral on 30 May 1980 provides a majestic backdrop to a Swindon built 3-car Inter-City unit (Class 120) as it leaves the city with the 11.30 Gloucester-Newport stopping service. *John Chalcraft*

Bristol-Gloucester

For the purpose of this title the NE/SW route really commences at Malago Vale Carriage Sidings to the west of Bristol Temple Meads station, it is at this point that a large number of the trains in use on the route and on Western Region services originating from Cheltenham, Hereford and Worcester are serviced, approaching Temple Meads northbound workings pass the Carriage Washing Plant at Bedminster before curving beneath the Bath Road bridge to pass alongside Bath Road Depot before entering the cavernous interior of the station's all over roof, with the introduction of HSTs on the main line to Paddington, Bath Roads tasks have been minimised although the amount of stone traffic now generated within the area has led to the allocation of '37s' from South Wales to the depot. The depot also provides motive power for trains to Weymouth normally '31s' and services the Class 33s in use on the Bristol-Portsmouth workings, as with Cardiff Canton the majority of NE/SW workings are normally handled by locomotives which originate outside the area.

From Temple Meads the line diverges from the main route to London at Bristol East junction to run parallel to the South Wales route through Lawrence Hill and Stapleton Road, up Filton bank to a point where the two routes diverge at Filton, the NE/SW taking the east chord of the triangle to join the main line from South Wales to Paddington just outside Bristol Parkway station. The two routes use common track until they pass over the former Midland route to the north at Westerleigh, at this point they diverge with the northbound route dropping down to take the old Midland route north through Wickwar Tunnel past Charfield to be joined by the ex-Western route across the Cotswolds at Standish junction. Until the closure of Eastgate station at Gloucester the two lines ran as a four track section until the ex-Midland route diverged, nowadays the lines converge to two tracks running into Gloucester via Gloucester Yard junction and Horton Road junction to pass the stabling point/mpd on the right before entering the long platform (designated Platforms 1 and 2) which acts as Gloucester's station.

Below: Malago Vale carriage sidings are situated 1½ miles to the west of Bristol Temple Meads station, they provide servicing facilities for locomotive hauled stock in the Bristol division as well as the stock used for Cheltenham and Worcester/Hereford services to Paddington, early on a winters morning No 50.002 *Superb* is accelerating the stock of the 08.15 Birmingham New Street-Plymouth as it heads west out of Bristol on 10 Feburary 1980. *John Chalcraft*

Left: The Southern Region's Class 33s have always been a wide ranging class despite their being confined to two depots, at the start of the summer 1980 services they ousted Bath Road's Class 31s from the Bristol-Portsmouth services, as a result they commenced regular duties to Weston-super-Mare with the 17.38 evening commuter service from Temple Meads, No. 33.012 heads west past Malago Vale on 24 July 1980. *John Chalcraft*

Centre left: A favourite spot for the visiting enthusiast to the Bristol area is Bedminster Park, where an excellent view can be obtained of trains leaving Temple Meads for the west, added interest is provided by trains passing through the Bristol carriage washing plant, on 12 April 1980 Class 46 No 46.009 accelerates a Saturday 'Adex' bound for the West Country past the park. *John Chalcraft*

Bottom left: A Panoramic view of Bristol Temple Meads and its environs in May 1977 showing the sharp curvature which hampers some operations in the vicinity of the station, the sidings to the right of the picture lead into Bath Road depot. No 45.003 is seen leaving the station and passing beneath the aptly named Bath Road Bridge. *John Chalcraft*

Top right: During the mid-1970s Class 25s were fairly common on summer Saturday trains to the South Devon resorts, but by the end of the decade their appearance had become something of a rarity. On 9 August 1980 Nos 25.261 and 25.267 restart the 12.23 Manchester Piccadilly-Paignton from its Temple Meads stop. *G Scott-Lowe*

Bottom right: On a November evening at Temple Meads the driver of No 47.088 *Samson* awaits departure time with the 18.30 HST substitute service to Paddington, at the time the train was composed of HST trailer stock with generator van for the provision of power to the heating and air conditioning services. *John Chalcraft*

Above: During 1979 Cardiff Canton received a number of Class 56s for heavy freight work including mgrs to Didcot, in September of the year members of the class were based at Swindon for crew training purposes. N 56.040 is pictured on 27 November 197 rounding the east chord of the triangle between North Somerset junction and Dr Days junction to gain the Badmintor route back to Swindon with the 10.08 Swindon Transfer-Swindon Transfer crew training special. *M. G. Miller*

Centre left: Laira based No 46.001 rounds the curve from Bristol East junction to Dr Days junction in June 1977 as it leaves Bristol at the head of the 08.15 Plymouth-Leeds. The trackbe of the former alignment (pre-1970) is visible to the left of the train, the locomotive and first coach being approximately level with the site of the old Dr Days Bridge Junction signalbox. *John Chalcraft*

Bottom left: Until January 1981 Lawrence Hill yards provided one of th few chances to see one of the rapidly diminishing Class 03 shunters at work i the south of England, but, in January the Avonside wharf branch which with its limited clearances was the only reason for the retention of the '03' was cleared for operation by the larger '08' class, the photograph taken on 19 May 1980 shows a very busy Lawrence Hill with No 03.382 fussing about its daily duties as No 31.238 prepares to leave with a train of vanfits, and No 47.086 *Colossus* is detached from a rake of Presflo cement wagons.
Graham Scott-Lowe

'ght: The only true suburban service ill existing in the Bristol area runs etween Bristol Temple Meads and evern Beach, on 22 October 1980 Class 21 single-car unit No W55033 leaves tapleton Road station with the 13.12 ervice to Severn Beach, the main line Bristol Parkway and South Wales our track) climbs away in the ackground, the single unit will diverge om the main line just before the verbridge at Narroways Hill nction. *John Chalcraft*

entre right: To the west of Bristol past arson Street Bristol possesses a small eightliner depot which effectively roduces one freightliner a day, the 3.30 Bristol West Depot-Glasgow ghthill, in the capable hands of 'Peak' o 45.019 the train climbs out of Bristol ast the junction at Narroways Hill with e single line branch to Avonmouth nd Severn Beach on 16 July 1980. The ranch is a useful diversionary route hich via Hallen Marsh junction will join the main route at Bristol arkway. *John Chalcraft*

ottom right: On a fine summer vening in July 1980 'Peak' No 45.051 ill displaying its original route dicator panels forges up Ashley Down ank out of Bristol towards Parkway ith the 19.34 Bristol-Newcastle 'ostal'. *John Chalcraft*

Above: A Royal occasion in June 1979 as the pride of the Western Region No 47.500 *Great Western* heads a slightly truncated Royal Train down Ashley Down bank into Bristol for servicing at Marsh Junction sidings.
John Chalcraft

Left: Class 31 No 31.320 drops down Ashley Down bank into Bristol past the remains of Ashley Down station with a Severn Tunnel Junction-Bristol East depot mixed freight on 25 May 1978. *John Chalcraft*

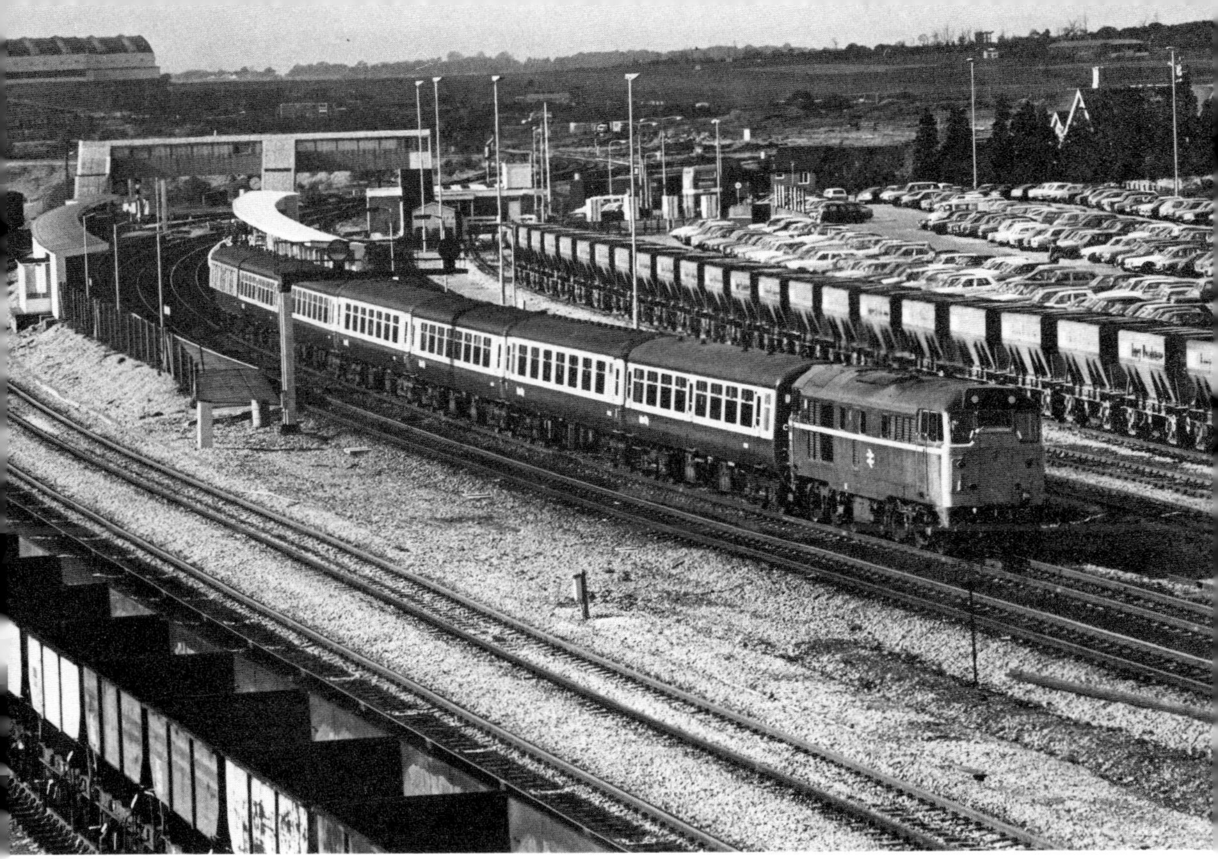

Above: At a time when larger powered locomotives of Class 46 were being withdrawn from service and put into 'temporary' store at Swindon it seems strange to find one of Old Oak Common's striped Class 31/4s No 31.412 already struggling to keep time on 29 October 1980 as it heads through Bristol Parkway with the 10.28 Taunton-Birmingham, on the skyline BAC's Filton Works and the Brabazon hangars can be clearly seen. *John Chalcraft*

Right: Although not on an approved route for the passage of steam locomotives on special trains the main Badminton route does see occasional visits by locomotives going to or from Swindon for attention or weighing, on 16 May 1979 No 6000 *King George V* was on test from Swindon to Swindon via Box and Badminton when photographed leaving Bristol Parkway past Stoke Gifford East. *M. G. Miller*

Left: Despite losing its main services in 1966 the old Midland main line into Bristol has remained in situ as a single track from Yate South junction as far as Westerleigh Yard. During winter 1978/79 the line received another uplift when it was taken over by the Bristol District Civil Engineer Dept and a training school for track maintenance purposes was established, on 27 February 1979 No 25.118 reverses a train of concrete sleepered track down the branch, in the background Westerleigh viaduct which carries the Bristol-Birmingham and South Wales-Paddington routes is clearly visible. *G. Scott-Lowe*

Centre left: A very grimy eth fitted Class 47 No 47.477 slows to join the Badminton route as it rounds the curve to Westerleigh junction with a train of anhydrous ammonia tanks bound for Fisons works at Avonmouth, the single mgr wagon is acting as a barrier vehicle in accordance with train operating instructions. *G. Scott-Lowe*

Bottom left: On a November day in 1980 while heading a northbound express Class 45 No 45.024 caught fire near Westerleigh, the train was stopped at Yate and the local Fire Brigade were summoned, it was found that the locomotive was unable to continue and another locomotive worked the train forward, the local firemen were still in attendance some hours later as a sister locomotive in somewhat better health draws a stone train from Tytherington onto the main line, it is of interest that the line from Yate Middle junction past Westerleigh junction is signalled for reversible working the stone train will not gain the down track until after Westerleigh junction on the main Badminton route. *G. Scott-Lowe*

Above: On 22 March 1980 No 47.146 curves away from the old Midland Railway route into Bristol at Yate South Junction, the locomotive is in fact travelling over what was once a single line (now doubled) linking the Midland main line with the Western Region's Paddington-South Wales route, the Midland route has now been singled to form a siding as far as the old Westerleigh Yard. *John Chalcraft*

Right: Despite their supposedly being 'non-standard' the Western Region's Class 52 diesel-hydraulics were recognised as being well suited to heavy freight haulage their last years often found them at work from both Merehead and Tytherington Quarries in the Bristol Division on stone haulage, on 14 July 1976 a grimy No D1072 *Western Glory* runs under the stone loading gantry at Tytherington. Tytherington Quarry itself was something of a surprise development in the mid-1970s it having been built upon the old Thornbury branch from Yate, complete tracklaying was necessary to handle the rail traffic the old branch line having been lifted some years earlier. *Graham Scott-Lowe*

Bottom right: The route from Bristol-Gloucester does not see a large amount of freight activity so the sight of Class 45 No 45.058 chattering a train of vanfits south from Charfield on 29 October 1980 was an unexpected bonus. *John Chalcraft*

Top: Motive power resources must have been stretched to the limit on Saturday 5 July as Class 50 No 50.007 *Hercules* finds itself off the normal rostered return working from Birmingham as it heads the 08.40 Liverpool Lime Street-Penzance south past Berkeley Road, in the background the Sharpness branch curves away to the left, this branch once linked east and west sides of the Severn via the old Severn railway bridge, the bridge was destroyed after a shipping accident in the 1960s although the branch remains to serve Sharpness Docks. *John Chalcraft*

Above: Some six miles south of Gloucester the main rail route through the Cotswolds joins the Bristol-Birmingham route, in this view the line curves in to join the NE/SW line, a 6-car rake of multiple-units led by No W51585 heads north on the 12 April 1980 with the 15.25 Bristol-Worcester. *Brian Morrison*

Above: The Gloucester-Swindon and Gloucester-Bristol routes diverge at Standish junction, on 5 July 1980 No 50.029 *Renown* diverges from the main line to take the cross Cotswold route via Stroud to Swindon at the head of the 08.31 Cheltenham-Paddington, later in the year this service became a casualty in the economy cuts a dmu providing a connecting service to Swindon. *John Chalcraft*

Top: Despite local opposition the old Midland Railway route into Gloucester Eastgate was closed with effect from 1 December 1975, the many level crossings upon the route were listed as one of the reasons for the change, on 5 March 1970 North British built Class 43 'Warship' diesel-hydraulic No 858 *Valorous* heads south out of Gloucester Eastgate with a Manchester-Plymouth train, at the time locomotive changing was taking place at Gloucester due to multi-aspect signalling work at Bristol. *N. E. Preedy*

Above: On 20 May 1973 Class 45 No 19 (now No 45.025) approaches Gloucester Eastgate under the Barton Street Crossing signal box to call at Eastgate's Platform 2, by this time the track to the old platform one had been lifted and traffic was being concentrated on Platforms 2 and 3. *N. E. Preedy*

Top: North British 'Warship' No 854 *Tiger* stands at Platform 2 of Gloucester Eastgate on 30 July 1971 at the head of the 11.20 Paignton-Manchester relief, the inclusion of Mk 1 stock in the old maroon livery indicates that coaching stock was at a premium, the lengthy covered footbridge linking the ex Midland Eastgate station and the ex Western Central station can be seen to the right of the locomotive. *David Wharton*

Above: From 1 December 1975 the old Midland route to Gloucester Eastgate was closed all traffic being concentrated on the ex-GW Central station where the platform had been lengthened to accommodate two trains at the same time, access to the station was via Gloucester Yard and Horton Road junctions, however, trains on the Bristol-Birmingham route are now forced to reverse after their Gloucester stop and the economics of this operation compared with the possible construction of a new station at Barnwood on the Gloucester avoiding line must be questionable, on 22 August 1979 No 08.849 ambles through the station with a Gloucester Docks-Gloucester Yard transfer freight as No 47.463 waits to leave the platform with a southbound express. *L. A. Nixon*

Gloucester-Birmingham

Trains leaving Gloucester for the north pass the stabling point on their left before diverging north at Horton Road junction to join the avoiding line at Barnwood junction, from Barnwood it is only a short distance before Cheltenham Spa is reached, the majority of trains now stop at this station with a multiple-unit link service providing a connection to Gloucester from trains avoiding that city.

From Cheltenham the line heads north through rural countryside passing Ashchurch, once the main line junction for branches to Tewkesbury and Evesham but little of the former splendour remains except the spur that leads into the local army depot, further north the majority of trains take the Worcester avoiding line at Abbotswood junction passing beneath the Oxford-Worcester route, trains stopping at Worcester diverge to the left, joining the route from Oxford at Norton junction, a large percentage of the freight traffic takes this route to reach Bescot. Worcester is now a comparatively unimportant railway centre although it still boasts two stations, the former sidings and yards are little used and the motive power depot has now been reduced to a roofless shell for the servicing of local diesel multiple-units and shunters, trains for Hereford diverge to the right after Shrub Hill station while northbound traffic plunges into a short tunnel as it heads for Droitwich. At Droitwich the main suburban route to Birmingham diverges to the left and this route is also taken by freight traffic for Bescot, the

Left: On 1 June 1980 Class 37 No 37.158 passes Horton Road depot and approaches Gloucester Central station with a train of empty ballast wagons for Tintern Quarry, behind the train the line diverging to the right is for Bristol and the south, while the train is coming off the line to Cheltenham and Birmingham. *N. E. Preedy*

Right: Gloucester was one of the last Western Region depots to use the shortlived 'D6300' class built by North British, No D6331 prepares to leave Gloucester yard with a local goods as No 6352 awaits its next duty, 16 July 1969, the last class members were withdrawn in January 1972 and no member completed 12 years service. *N. E. Preedy*

Bottom right: During the early 1970s Class 37 No 6941 (later 37.241) curves into Cheltenham Lansdown with a Severn Tunnel Junction-Bescot special freight, the line diverging to the right is the ex-GW main line to Honeybourne, Stratford-upon-Avon and Birmingham which was a prime diversionary route but has since been closed and lifted. The old Midland & South Western Joint line to Andover used to diverge to the left behind the signalbox which is just visible beyond the overbridge. *Barry J. Nicolle*

main line diverges to the right and the fact that it is single track as far as Stoke Works junction where it rejoins the main line is indicative of the importance now given to the Worcester connection by British Rail. Having rejoined the main line passenger trains normally accelerate to achieve maximum speed for the climb from Bromsgrove to Blackwell up the two miles at 1 in 37 that constitute the Lickey Incline, trains that stop at Bromsgrove normally grind their way up the gradient at little more than walking pace while the few mixed freights normally take the two Class 37 bankers to provide assistance to the summit. Once over the summit at Blackwell locomotives have a comparatively easy task as they run into Birmingham past the junction station at Barnt Green where the Redditch branch diverges and through the suburbs of Longbridge and Northfields to Kings Norton, where freight traffic normally diverges to the right to avoid the New Street complex rejoining the main line at Landor Street junction, passenger traffic diverges left to take the line through Bournville, Selly Oak, University and Fiveways stations before diving into the tunnels under the city centre and emerging in the concrete jungle that is New Street station, it is on this last section that many delays can occur due to the considerable amount of suburban traffic using the same tracks into the city.

Left: Station personnel await the departure of the 07.30 Swansea-Leeds from Cheltenham on 30 May 1980 as Class 31 No 31.299 rumbles through with a Bescot-Severn Tunnel mixed freight. *John Chalcraft*

Below: A train of empty bogie bolster wagons is accelerated round the curve through Cheltenham by Class 25 No 25.138 on 25 July 1980. At one time Cheltenham could boast three stations but with the closure of the ex-GW Honeybourne route to Birmingham only one station now remains this being positioned on the ex-Midland route to the north and formerly known as Cheltenham Lansdown. *N. E. Preedy*

Top right: Shortly after returning from works attention an extremely weak Class 50 No 50.002 *Superb* struggles to restart the 06.26 Plymouth-Liverpool away from Cheltenham Spa on 10 January 1980. This train is normally rostered for '50' haulage as far as Birmingham providing the only regular working over the complete route. A 3-car dmu awaits departure with the 09.50 Cheltenham-Swindon from the other platform. *John Chalcraft*

Bottom right: To the north of Cheltenham lies a coal concentration depot which has survived the economy ravages of the 1960s and still maintains a direct rail link, on 1 February 1981 the two depot shunters lie at rest, the shed to the left is all that remains of the High Street goods shed. *B. J. Nicolle*

Left: Some 18 miles north of Cheltenham lies Abbotswood junction where the line into Worcester diverges from the main route, regaining the main at Stoke Works junction, despite the Worcester catchment area the majority of trains now bypass the City, just round the curve from Abbotswood lies Norton junction where the route into Worcester joins the Oxford-Worcester line. On 15 June 1980 No 45.010 negotiates the junction past the signalbox with 8Z43 the 15.15 Severn Tunnel-Bescot freight, a refurbished Metro-Cammell 3-car dmu heads south with the 17.21 Worcester-Gloucester. *John Chalcraft*

Below: Eth fitted class 47 No 47.484 *Isambard Kingdom Brunel* comes off the single line Oxford-Worcester route on 13 June 1980 at the head of the 15.00 Paddington-Hereford at Norton junction despite the fact that for operating purposes the route is now of a minor nature old habits die hard the local railmen still referring to it as the 'main' with the Abbotswood line being the 'branch'. *John Chalcraft*

Right: Worcester Shrub Hill is but a shadow of its former self having lost many of its prime services, in March 1979 a Class 45 curves the 04.24 Stoke-St Blazey 'Clayliner' through the station under the parcels bridge. *J. G. Glover*

Centre right: A very interesting photograph showing Worcester motive power depot open day on 12 April 1969, note that the vast majority of the motive power present represents locomotive classes since rendered extinct. *British Rail*

Bottom right: On a very cold October 1980 morning, a wisp of steam rises from the steam heating boiler of No 46.007 as it rounds the curve into Droitwich Spa with the 06.32 Leeds-Paignton, the train has just passed over the single track section from Stoke Works junction, the line diverging to the left past the signalbox leads to Birmingham via Stourbridge. *John Chalcraft*

Left: An interesting photograph included for comparison purposes and showing the mid-1960s scene at Bromsgrove after the elimination of steam and before the installation of colour light signalling, a Class 35 ('Hymek') No 7048 in blue livery passes on the slow line with a train of vans, a Class 25 waits at the signals while its train brakes are unpinned, three Class 37s are being used to offer banking assistance. *A. A. Vickers*

Below: The modern look at Bromsgrove after resignalling and track rationalisation eth 'Peak' No 45.104 *The Royal Warwickshire Fusiliers* at the head of the 13.35 Glasgow-Taunton passes two very scruffy Class 37s (No 37.232 and 37.138) as they await their next banking duty 13 June 1980. *John Chalcraft*

Right: During the late 1970s the 15.07 Plymouth-Manchester became something of an institution with enthusiasts in the Gloucester area as it invariably produced small motive power for haulage during summer months, on 13 June 1980, Class 20s were turned out for the duty, Nos 20.140 and 20.192 were thought incapable of a single handed assault on the Lickey and assistance was offered in the form of the two bankers Nos 37.232 and 37.138, with this 5,500hp combination and the front coaches full of enthusiasts, the bank was climbed in a somewhat noisy style. *John Chalcraft*

Below: Another interesting photograph included for comparison purposes and showing the top of the Lickey Incline on 29 March 1967 as a Swindon built (now Class 120) 3-car unit in blue livery and with small yellow warning panel starts the descent towards Bromsgrove, the semaphore signals, signalbox and up platform are now all memories of the railway scene. *A. A. Vickers*

Left; top and bottom: As the photographer arrived at Blackwell on 3 February 1981 the noise from some way down the Lickey Incline indicated that the 09.35 Cardiff Tidal Sidings-Scunthorpe was making a steady if somewhat slow ascent, a minute later a pair of Class 20s Nos 20.069 and 20.148 clambered over the summit, the photograph was taken from the site of the former Blackwell station up platform, seconds later the Lickey bankers appeared in the form of '37s' Nos 37.224 and 37.241 and were photographed dropping away from the brake van at the rear of the train. *John Chalcraft*

Right: A Class 117 3-car dmu based in Bristol is framed by the overbridge which crosses the Redditch branch tracks at Barnt Green as it heads the 17.05 Birmingham-Worcester service, June 1977. *John Glover*

Centre right: In the shadow of British Leylands Longbridge Works on 12 July 1980 a Tyseley based Metro-Cammell 3-car unit led by No M50315 approaches Longbridge station with the 10.22 Worcester Shrub Hill-Four Oaks service. *John Chalcraft*

Bottom right: Young spotters watch as one of Landore depot's steam heated Class 37s No 37.184 powers out of Birmingham past the partially built Longbridge station on 12 July 1980 with the 08.30 Manchester Piccadilly-Swansea service, this service provides the return working for the locomotive from the 06.55 Gloucester-Birmingham service and often produces 'smaller power'. *John Chalcraft*

Left: The prototype (or was it DP2?) Class 50 now No 50.050 *Fearless* hurries into Birmingham past the scaffolding of Longbridge's new station as it heads the 06.26 Plymouth-Liverpool on the last leg of its diesel hauled journey on 12 July 1980. The train will take electric power for the remainder of its journey from New Street. *John Chalcraft*

Centre left: The rostered return working of the Class 50 from the 06.26 ex Plymouth is the 10.23 Manchester Piccadilly-Plymouth, in deep January snow No 50.003 *Temeraire* rounds the sharp Lifford curve as it accelerates the train out of Birmingham past Kings Norton, the line in the foreground is the Birmingham avoiding line (which incorporates the infamous Camp Hill Incline) which rejoins the main line to the north at Landor Street junction, Saltley and is an important freight route. *K. Connolly*

Bottom left: Certain freight workings around Birmingham using the 'Camp Hill' line take banking assistance for the climb from Saltley towards Kings Norton, on 13 May 1977 Class 25 No 25.038 assists a southbound freight past Bordesley junction. *K. Connolly*

Top right: Another photograph taken at Bordesley junction on the same date with the floodlights of Birmingham City's St Andrews football ground in the background as Class 31 No 31.134 heads a southbound train of strip steel, the locomotive is one of the earlier examples of Class 31 without the roof mounted train describer panels, the line diverging to the right leads to Bordesley South junction and the ex-Great Western route to Banbury and Oxford. *K. Connolly*

Bottom right: St Andrews junction lies just below the ground of Birmingham City FC, on 11 November 1976, 'Peak' Class 45 No 45.006 *Honourable Artillery Company* eases a northbound train of coal from South Wales over the junction towards Saltley, the line diverging to the right leads to Grand junction and ultimately New Street station. *P. D. Hawkins*

Above: The improvements in suburban services in the Birmingham area led to the building/rebuilding of several stations one of these stations being situated to serve the Queen Elizabeth Hospital/University complex to the south-west of the city centre and not surprisingly called 'University', a Derby Works Class 116 3-car suburban unit leaves the station and runs alongside the Worcester and Birmingham canal in surprisingly rural surroundings with a Longbridge-Sutton Coldfield service, May 1978. *J. G. Glover*

Left: Fiveways station is built on the site of an earlier station closed in the 1950s, on 16 June 1979 two Class 116/3-car suburban units on services to Lichfield City and Longbridge pass in the station. *John Chalcraft*

Droitwich-Bescot-Lichfield City-Wichnor junction

Special mention is made of this primarily freight route due to its importance in the operation of the NE/SW freight traffic, as already stated the majority of wagonload traffic diverges from the main line at Abbotswood junction, passes through Worcester and diverges at Droitwich to take the suburban route via Kidderminster and Stourbridge Junction, at Stourbridge the passenger route diverges to take the route through Rowley Regis to New Street, freight working takes the route past Round Oak Steelworks, beneath Dudley and past the Freightliner terminal before dropping down to pass beneath the electrified Birmingham-Wolverhampton route at Tipton and eventually enter Bescot yard at its west end beneath the M6 motorway. Wagonload traffic is normally sorted at Bescot before resuming its journey.

From the yard traffic once again uses the exit at the west end to gain the line to Walsall, sharing the line with the 25kV multiple-units on local suburban services, the electrification ending at Walsall, but, freight traffic continuing north to Lichfield where one of the local passenger services converges from the right as the line approaches Lichfield City station, the suburban service terminating at Lichfield, the freight traffic continuing north passing over the West Coast main line at Lichfield Trent Valley to regain the main NE/SW route at Wichnor junction south of Burton-on-Trent.

Below: Prime freight movement on the route travels round Birmingham on two routes, the second of the routes being via Worcester, Droitwich Spa, Stourbridge Junction and the freight only route through Dudley to Bescot, on 30 October 1980 refurbished Class 116 No M50872 waits at Stourbridge Junction with a Birmingham bound local as Class 122 No M55009 approaches on a local train from the short Stourbridge Town branch, the semaphore signal on the branch remains but the semaphores on the main line have just been replaced by colour light signals.
John Chalcraft

Top: Sulzer Type 2 No 25.212 accelerates a train of coal empties from Shut End coal depot at Pensnett south through Stourbridge Junction on 30 October 1980 past the ex-GW signalbox which remains operational despite the replacement of local semaphore signals by colour lights, a Class 20 stands in the yard on an engineers' train. *John Chalcraft*

Above: Dudley, situated in the heart of the industrial black country boasts a large freightliner terminal, on a sunny February morning Class 25 No 25.289 has just reversed its short train out from the depot onto the main line to commence the journey to Nottingham with the 10.55 Freightliner service. *John Chalcraft*

Top: Under the wires at the west end of Bescot yards, Class 46 'Peak' No 46.025 passes a Class 45 and an '85' electric as it heads the 13.35 Bescot-Gloucester freight past Bescot mpd on 7 July 1976. *K. Connolly*

Above: A derailment between Bescot and Dudley on 30 October 1980 caused considerable operating problems for freight services in the Birmingham area, Class 25 No 25.271 was photographed leaving Bescot (with the station and mpd in the background) with a short engineers' train.
John Chalcraft

Left: Class 56s are now common power on the freight line from Bescot to Wichnor junction via Walsall, but on 1 September 1977, when No 56.033 was photographed passing Walsall with a load of empty mgr wagons the class was still something of a novelty in the area, at the time the locomotive was based at Saltley for crew training purposes and one of its frequent duties was an mgr train to Buildwas, the train originated at Kingsbury. The route via Bescot to Wichnor junction is also used by passenger trains on the route when necessitated by Sunday diversions. *A. J. Whitehouse*

Centre left: Lichfield City lies at the northern end of the cross-Birmingham suburban service from Redditch and Longbridge, it is also positioned on the freight route from Wichnor junction to Bescot, on 12 August 1980 a 3-car unit is in the process of being stabled in the sidings as Class 20s Nos 20.075 and 20.047 double-head a mixed freight from Toton to Bescot through the station. *John Chalcraft*

Bottom left: Continuous welded track seems to be something of a luxury on a line used for little else than freight traffic, Class 25 No 25.053 ambles past Lichfield and is about to pass over the West Coast main line at Lichfield Trent Valley as it heads the 10.55 Dudley-Nottingham freightliner on 12 August 1980. *John Chalcraft*

Right: With a clear road No 25.143 heads a northbound mixed freight past Lichfield Trent Valley junction on 12 August 1980. The signal immediately behind the locomotive is situated on the steep and sharply curved spur from the high level freight route to the West Coast main line and is regularly traversed by the loaded mgr trains to Rugeley power station, the small platform on the high level line is all that remains of the Lichfield Trent Valley High Level platforms. *John Chalcraft*

35
X15
95B

Birmingham-Derby

As already stated Birmingham's New Street station lies virtually beneath the city centre and northbound traffic leaves the station through tunnels, the same tunnels carry the electrified route to Euston, the main line to Banbury and the suburban route to Lichfield all routes diverge from each other within two miles of the station, the main line to the north burrowing beneath the main line to Rugby and Euston to emerge alongside Birmingham Freightliner depot, the predominantly freight line from Kings Norton converging on the right and joining the route at Landor Street junction and the main servicing depot for the area, Saltley, lies back behind the junction, yet again the depot has no allocation of its own (other than shunters) but often houses a wide range of locomotives from depots as far apart as Laira (Plymouth), Old Oak Common, March and Gateshead.

Once past Saltley the track is quadrupled to pass through the extensive marshalling yards at Washwood Heath, Metropolitan-Cammell's works, the birthplace of a large number of our existing diesel multiple-units can be seen on the right, normally with many railway vehicles and buses being visible. From beyond Washwood Heath the line passes beneath the northbound M6 passing Castle Bromwich junction and eventually reaching Water Orton, to the east of Water Orton the main route diverges to the left from the line to Nuneaton and Leicester passing the large Hams Hall power station, the predominantly freight line via Whitacre junction eventually rejoins the main route at Kingsbury South junction and some two miles further north the freight branches to Birch Coppice and Baddesley Collieries diverge to the right. Beyond Kingsbury the route heads almost due north passing through the middle of extensive quarry workings before reaching Wilnecote and eventually the once important railway interchange point of Tamworth.

Before the completion of the West Coast main line electrification Tamworth was a major interchange point for postal traffic between the WCML and the NE/SW route, however with the completion of the Birmingham New Street rebuilding the majority of this work was moved to New Street, beyond Tamworth the route travels across the flood plain of the River Trent on a low embankment passing Wichnor junction where the freight line from Bescot joins the route. The sizeable Drakelow power station is the next visible feature on the line although supplied by mgr trains the entrance to the station is off the freight only line to Coalville and is not directly visible, Branston junction is the point at which the main and freight lines diverge, the junction is almost opposite the small two road engine shed which supplied fuel to locomotives operating out of Burton, on both sides of Burton station extensive signs of the once thriving rail connections into the local breweries exist although the majority of these spurs have now been lifted.

To the north of the remodelled Burton station lie the extensive Wetmore sidings where large numbers of mgr coal hoppers are held prior to maintenance, the line then runs parallel to the River Trent to Willington where the old North Staffordshire line from Stoke converges on the left, at Stenson North Staffs junction, to the right lie the extensive sidings belonging to CEGB's Willington power station, which currently receives its coal by wagonload although it is shortly to be converted to operate on the Merry Go Round system, immediately to the north of Willington the freight line to Trent and Toton diverges to the right at Stenson junction, the main line continuing into the Derby suburbs passing the suburban station at Peartree before joining the main line from London at the south end of Derby station. The main refuelling point is now situated alongside the BREL works at Derby, but locomotives are normally found stabled on the curve parallel with the London line, the carriage works lie on the right hand side before the junction but little is visible, a glimpse of the stock belonging to the research centre is normally possible at its base alongside the London line, and the locomotive works lie to the right of the station. The station has been the cause of some concern for several years and is a candidate for early rebuilding although its exterior facade will probably be retained.

Top left: Both entrances to Birmingham New Street station are through tunnels beneath the city centre, on 28 October 1978 'Peak' Class 46 No 46.018 emerges from the catacomb and approaches the city with the 09.40 Cardiff-Newcastle, Class 86 electric No 86.034 stands in the sidings alongside the Birmingham power box. *A. O. Wynn*

Bottom left: Empty stock can be held at a variety of points within the Birmingham area but a system of loop lines and junctions around the city enables fairly easy access for incoming ecs to New Street station, on 12 July 1980. Thornaby depot's No 37.003 approaches New Street at the head of the incoming ecs for the 09.35 (SO) service to Scarborough. *John Chalcraft*

Left: During the 1970s the lumbering shape of the early modernisation plan diesels built by English Electric and now classified as Class 40s has had few (if any) regular workings into Birmingham on passenger traffic although at times o pressure their appearance on workings from both the north-east or north-west has not been uncommon, on 5 March 1979 Holbeck depot turned out No 40.107 to work the 14.39 Leeds-Plymouth it was pictured at New Street prior to departure for Gloucester. *K. Connolly*

Below: Two forms of British Rail motive power meet at Birmingham New Street on 2 August 1980, in the form of the diesel-electric locomotive which generates its own electricity to provide power to its traction motors and the ac electric locomotive which uses the 25kV overhead power supply system, one of the Western Region's Class 50s No 50.001 *Dreadnought* waits in the centre road for the arrival of its train as Class 86 electric No 86.242 prepares to leave with a train for the north-west. *John Chalcraft*

Right: Class 56 freight locos have seen very little work on passenger services, but, they are occasionally utilised as motive power when Sunday engineering work necessitates the switching off of power on the main Birmingham-Rugby route. Sunday 3 August 1980 found two Class 56s in use between Birmingham and Nuneaton No 56.052 was photographed dragging Class 87 No 87.027 out of New Street at the head of the 09.00 Wolverhampton-Euston. *Kevin Connolly*

Centre right: To the east of New Street the main line dives under the main electrified route to London at Grand Junction to join the main Birmingham avoiding line at Landor Street junction with Birmingham Freightliner Terminal on the left and Saltley motive power depot on the right. On 30 October 1980 No 40.129 eases the 14.45 Birmingham FLT-Holyhead out of the Freightliner terminal, the train will leave the north-east main line at Castle Bromwich junction (beyond Washwood Heath Yards) to take the freight only route to Ryecroft junction, Walsall, it will then travel via Bushbury junction to gain the main line to Crewe and Holyhead. *John Chalcraft*

Bottom right: 'Peak' Class 46 No 139 (now 46.002) eases its train past Saltley motive power depot as it joins the main line at Landor Street junction, the semaphores controlling the entrance to the freightliner depot have now been replaced by colour lights, the date is 23 July 1973. *K. Connolly*

.eft: British Rail's latest aquisition the :lass 56 heavy freight locomotives are ıow well represented on workings hrough the Birmingham area, the najority of these workings comprising Merry Go Round' coal workings from ne Nottinghamshire pits to Didcot ower station, the trains enter irmingham via Water Orton and liverge from the main line outside altley depot to gain the ex Western Region route out of the city past Tyseley ia Landor Street and Bordesley unctions, on 3 February 1981 one of the ater series '56s' (with revised cab detail) Jo 56.059 passes Washwood Heath ards with return mgr empties. *John Chalcraft*

ottom left: On 3 February 1981 the hatter of No 25.184 as it leaves Vashwood Heath yards disturbs cavenging gulls on one of the local actory dumps, in the yard an nidentified Class 56 stables the stock of n mgr train. *John Chalcraft*

op right: The M6 motorway crosses he main rail route to the north between Vater Orton and Washwood Heath, on 3 ebruary 1981 non-boilered No 47.321 repares to pick up an oil train from the idings beneath the motorway as '20's Jo 20.141 and 20.090 amble back to altley their day's work omplete. *John Chalcraft*

entre right: Water Orton station onsists of an island platform with two acks passing on either side of the sland, on 27 May 1980 snowplough tted No 25.305 passes the station light ngine as it heads into irmingham. *John Chalcraft*

ottom right: On 27 May 1980 No. 5.213 chatters over the junction with he Derby line as it approaches Water Orton with a cement train from the eicester direction, the signalbox is now n use as a pw store having been endered redundant with the opening of he Saltley power box in 1969. *John Chalcraft*

Left: 'Peak' class No 45.047 clatters over the junction with the Leicester line as it approaches Water Orton and Birmingham with a summer Saturday Sheffield-Paignton train, the CEGB's Hams Hall power station cooling towers stand on the skyline, this locomotive was to be one of the first Class 45 casualties caused by the recession of the early 1980s. *John Chalcraft*

Centre left: During late 1979 and part of 1980 the main line from Water Orton to Kingsbury South junction was closed for complete rebuilding and relaying the majority of traffic being diverted over the normally freight only line from Kingsbury South to Whitacre Junction where the Nuneaton-Birmingham route was gained, on 27 May 1980 Class No 31.188 approaches Water Orton from the Nuneaton line with block working of strip-steel flats, the extensive nature of the engineering work can be gauged from the view of the main route diverging to the left. *John Chalcraft*

Bottom left: 27 May 1980 was a bitterly cold day and the only locomotive apparently available in Birmingham to propel the 11.35 Poole-Leeds/Newcastle forward from New Street was non-boilered ex works No 37.143, through passengers apparently had a very cold journey as it was reported that a Class 56 worked the train from Reading to Birmingham due to further shortages of power, the train was photographed approaching Whitacre junction. *John Chalcraft*

Top right: During the summer timetable of 1980 the 09.50 Norwich-Birmingham was diagrammed for haulage by two Class 31s on Saturdays, the load being strengthened to 10 coaches, on 16 August 1980 Nos 31.313 and 31.176 weave the train off the Nuneaton line through the remains of the platforms at Whitacre junction. *S. J. Turner*

Bottom right: The crew of No 25.263 working a short pick up freight on 5 May 1980 await the passage of No 47.112 on a diverted relief working from the north to Birmingham at Whitacre junction, the passenger working having just traversed the freight only route from Kingsbury South junction to Whitacre due to the rebuilding of the normal direct route to Water Orton. *John Chalcraft*

Left: The driver of No 47.041 anxiously leans out of the cab window to check that all is clear as he commences the reversal of his train of oil tanks from Kingsbury Shunting Frame into the local oil terminal on 27 May 1980. The junction also provides access to the branch which leads to Birch Coppice and Baddesley Collieries.
John Chalcraft

Below: With hoar-frost on both track and hedgerows on 4 December 1976 a pair of Class 20s Nos 20.174 and 20.066 commence the run down to the branch from Baddesley Colliery to Kingsbury North junction with an unfitted coal train. *C. R. Davis*

Left: Panic on the platform at Tamworth on 28 June 1980 as 'Peak' No 45.059 shows all the signs of over-running with the 07.50 Leeds-Weymouth, a hard brake application ensured that all passengers joined the train safely, the two towers on the up platform are the enginehouses for the lifts linking the ex Midland route to the West Coast main line on the lower level, they now see little use compared with the time when the station was a major mail interchange point between the two routes. *John Chalcraft*

Above: The old order on the route, although never in regular use the Class 40s have made numerous appearances normally at times of locomotive shortages, No 40.012 still showing the bolts where its *Aureol* nameplates should be fixed approaches Wichnor Junction with the 08.17 Leeds-Poole on [illegible] November 1978. Normally the train combines with the 06.56 Newcastle-Poole at Sheffield but due to late running by the latter portion the Leeds portion was sent forward by itself on this occasion. *A. O. Wynn*

Right: A grimy Western Region Class 37 No 37.274 accelerates a train of oil tank wagons south away from Burton past Branston junction on 12 August 1980, the junction provides access to the freight only lines and many collieries in the Coalville area. *John Chalcraft*

Left: During the last days of steam, Burton could boast a depot with quite a large allocation of locomotives, since dieselisation the old shed buildings have been demolished and replaced by a two road refuelling shed, at the start of the 1970s up to 20 locomotives of predominantly Class 20 could be found here at weekends between duties but by 1980 four or five locos had become the norm with the majority of locomotives associated with local freight working being stabled at Coalville, on 28 June 1980 No 47.281 ambles past with a Saturday mgr working, No 56.050 stands outside the shed while No 08.623 awaits refuelling. The depot was finally closed in Autumn 1981.
John Chalcraft

Centre left: When the 'Peak' class diesel locomotives were introduced they were hailed as the highest powered diesel locos on British Railways and hauled main line expresses on the West Coast main line, some years later in the 1960s the first 10 locos of the class, numbered D1-D10, were re-allocated to Toton Depot, their train heating boilers were isolated and later removed and they were relegated to freight work, during 1969 No D7 (later 44.007) still sporting its *Ingleborough* nameplates heads a mixed freight north through Burton.
A. O. Wynn

Bottom left: During the mid 1970s overhaul of the Western Region's Class 50s was transferred from BREL Crewe to BREL Doncaster works, for the first couple of years locomotives were normally transferred 'dead on own wheels' to the works, but during 1979 crews were trained on the locomotives to enable their transfer to and from works on regular service trains, probably the most likely train to produce such workings was the Edinburgh-Plymouth, on 2 June 1980 No 50.011 *Centurion* approaches Burton with the southbound service.
A. O. Wynn

Right: The route from Derby to Birmingham sees many test trains in conjunction with the work of the Railway Technical Centre at Derby, on 29 June 1979 Brush Class 47/7 (converted from Class 47/4) No 47.704 *Dunedin* propels the first of the push-pull train sets destined for the Edinburgh-Glasgow service out of Burton as it returns to Derby after testing. *A. O. Wynn*

Below: Burton has long been associated with the brewing business and sidings still run directly from the main line into the brewery, trip freight working into the brewery is normally handled by one of Burton's 'O8' shunters, however on 30 April 1979 Class 20 No 20.174 was deputising for the normal power as it shunted malt hoppers at the Ind Coope Burton brewery sidings, the rebuilt Burton station can be seen in the top right hand corner of the picture. *A. O. Wynn*

Left: One of the daily trip freight workings in Burton conveys 'green carded' wagons from Drakelow CEGB sidings to Wetmore sidings for attention on 1 August 1977 No 08.623 rumbles past the old goods yard sidings (now lifted) en route to Wetmore sidings. *A. O. Wynn*

Bottom left: Midway between Burton and Derby lies Stenson North Staffs junction where the main traffic flow is joined by the cross-country route from Crewe to Derby, on 18 July 1979 No 40.100 is captured to the north of the junction as it drags Nos 25.166 and 25.167 towards Derby for attention. *A. O. Wynn*

Top right: Immediately opposite Stenson North Staffs junction lies the large coalfired CEGB Willington power station, on 12 August 1980 Class 20s Nos 20.070 and 20.077 enter the station yard with an unfitted coal train, in the background one of the three remaining Class 44s No 44.007 prepares to leave the yard with a freight for Toton, the main line is visible to the right. *John Chalcraft*

Centre right: A familiar sight on the main line at North Staffs junction are trains being run from the Railway Technical Centre to its test track which is situated off the Crewe line at Egginton junction, the RTC's Class 24 No 968007 (now 97201 *Experiment*) heads a small train away from Derby with an easy load on 20 July 1977. *D. Clow*

Bottom right: Just north of Willington power station lies Stenson junction where the freight only route to Toton yard via Trent diverges from the main line to the north, on 12 August 1980, one of the last three Class 44 'Peaks' No 44.007 (minus *Ingleborough* nameplates) and appearing to be in run down condition takes the freight route with a Willington power station-Toton train of coal empties, this 'Peak,' sub class was rendered extinct in main line service in November 1980 after 21 years service. *John Chalcraft*

Left: In place of the more normal motive power Class 31s Nos 31.117 and 31.149 accelerate out of Derby with the 10.10 Newcastle-Cardiff, the two locomotives make interesting comparison as despite their being members of the same class cab detail differences are apparent, the leading loco being one of the earlier batch with train indicator disks, the second loco has the roof mounted train indicator panel fitted to later locomotives, 5 August 1978.
L. A. Nixon

Centre left: Derby Carriage Works carry out major overhaul on locomotive hauled stock from the majority of BR's Regions, on 4 August 1980 Brush Type 2 No 31.135 has just arrived from the Western Region with Mk 2 stock and a brakevan requiring attention, having run into the yard alongside the station it will reverse the stock across the junction and into Litchurch Lane works yard. Access to the works being via the small underbridge just visible in the photograph behind the semaphore shunting signal (above the first coach). *John Chalcraft*

Bottom left: Despite the fact that the majority of track in the Derby area is controlled from Derby power box some semaphore signals remain, on 4 August 1980 a shabby Class 20 No 20.063 prepares to negotiate the tight curve into the works yard with a transfer freight from Chaddesden Sidings. *John Chalcraft*

Top right: Class 20s see regular employment on summer Saturday passenger trains to and from Skegness although their use on other passenger workings in the Derby area is something of a rarity, on 22 July 1978 the Class 47 working the 08.34 Leeds-Paignton was declared a failure at Derby, the only other locos available were Nos 20.188 and 20.009 and these were entrusted with the working as far as Gloucester. *Kevin Connolly*

Bottom right: Ex works coaching stock from Derby Litchurch Lane is often attached to the rear of service trains for transfer to its own Region, on 12 May 1979 Derby station pilot No 08.303 gingerly approaches the rear of a northbound train with a Mk 2F coach for attachment. *A. O. Wynn*

20188

Above: Derby station is a candidate for remodelling and rebuilding although in the current economic climate an early start on work seems unlikely, on 4 August 1980 the driver of eth 'Peak' No 45.104 heading the 12.10 Sheffield-St Pancras engages a young enthusiast in conversation. *John Chalcraft*

Derby-Sheffield

As the train leaves Derby in a northbound direction it passes over the River Derwent, and it is this river and its valley which form the natural contours which the railway uses for the next 12 miles. Some 1½ miles north of Derby station St Mary's Yard is passed on the left, this yard appears to be used as a collecting point for items used in conjunction with the Railway Technical Centre and in the early 1980s several of the trailer cars for the old 'Blue Pullman' units and High Density emu prototype No 4002 were present, a short distance further and the line runs into open countryside and passes Little Eaton junction (on right) where the short branch to the mine at Denby diverges. From Little Eaton it is a short distance to the small town of Duffield which still boasts the remains of a station and a rail link to Derby, at this point another branch which owes its existence to local quarrying diverges to the left to thread its way up a river valley to the limestone quarry at Wirksworth. Shortly after passing Duffield the line plunges into Milford Tunnel beneath one of the eastern flanks of the Pennines to emerge alongside the Derwent which it then crosses before passing beneath the streets of Belper to recross the meandering Derwent four times before reaching the junction at Ambergate, it is at this point that the truncated remains of the former Midland main line diverge to the left to reach its current terminus at Matlock. The main line now dives through the short Ambergate Tunnel to travel along the valley of the River Amber (tributary of the Derwent) with the Pennine flank to the left, plunging into a deep cutting before passing beneath Clay Cross in the mile long Clay Cross tunnel and emerging at the junction with the Erewash Valley route from Nottingham and Toton.

The Erewash valley route is quadruple track with two tracks primarily used for freight purposes, this system is retained until Tapton junction is reached to the north of Chesterfield where the freight and passenger lines diverge, the freight route following the valley of the River Rother via Staveley.

At the present time the most immediately noticeable feature of operation on the freight route is the existence of semaphore signalling, until recently the complete route as far as Rotherham was operated in this manner, but, the northern part of the route from Rotherham as far as Treeton junction has now been converted to colour light, cable laying is in progress in the area near Beighton junction and life expectancy of the remaining semaphores in the area must be short. At Staveley the line passes close to the old Barrow Hill depot which is visible from the line, the depot is probably the last true roundhouse in day to day use for the purpose for which it was built, beyond Staveley the line passes through the South Yorkshire coalfield and a large number of collieries with their associated trackwork are visible. At Beighton junction diverted passenger trains diverge from the freight line to take the old GC route into Sheffield passing through Woodhouse, Darnall and gaining Sheffield Midland via Nunnery junction. The last five miles of this route are currently travelled beneath the catenary of the now closed 1,500V dc ex-GC route across the Pennines to Manchester. Freight traffic from Beighton junction passes beneath the Sheffield-Worksop route before reaching Treeton junction where the line to Tinsley Yard (east end) diverges to the left at Treeton South junction, other traffic continues north with northbound traffic from Tinsley joining the route at Treeton North Junction to continue to Rotherham where the main passenger route is joined.

From Tapton junction at Chesterfield the passenger route diverges from the freight in a north-westerly direction passing the large scrapyard at Old Whittington on the right, the yard was responsible for the demise of many steam engines and in recent years, diesel locos, diesel multiple-units and more recently Southern Region de-icing units have met their fate in the yard. After Whittington the line passes through predominantly hilly countryside before reaching Dronfield, it is the nature of the country and the acceptance by North Derbyshire Council that rail as an effective means of transport is an asset to the community that led to the re-opening of Dronfield station in January 1981 to provide peak services to and from Chesterfield and Sheffield.

After leaving Dronfield the line dives into the mile long Bradway tunnel before emerging into the Sheffield suburb of Dore, shortly after emerging from the tunnel the chord line to the Hope Valley route diverges to the left and the main link to the Hope valley from Sheffield diverges at Hope station, the final four miles into Sheffield pass the remains of Millhouses station and the former Midland depot before passing through a short tunnel to emerge in Sheffield Midland station.

Above: An interesting photograph for comparison purposes showing Derby station north signal box and the superb gantry of semaphore signals that guarded the northern station approaches before the installation of colour light signalling. In old livery before the adoption of a new British Rail logo and colour scheme 'Peak' No. D39 (now 45 033) is seen approaching the station with a train from Leeds on 10 March 1963. *P. H. Wells*

Left: Another interesting historic photograph taken at Derby on 23 July 1962 shows Beyer Peacock 'Hymek' diesel-hydraulic on test from its birthplace at Beyer Peacock's Manchester works before final painting, the locomotive (No D7046) is in grey works primer and has worked to Derby over the former Midland main line to Manchester (via Matlock), the line was truncated some years later leaving only the Matlock branch and the predominantly freight lines in the Peak Forest/Buxton area as a remnant of a former main line. *P. J. Lynch*

Derby Works

From a position where Derby locomotive works were once full of locomotives of Classes 45, 46 and 25 under construction in the early and middle sixties their work load has almost gone full circle, with very few locos now being present for overhaul purposes but an increasing number of HST power cars undergoing attention, members of Class 45 and 46 still receive attention although the Class 45/1 (eth) classification is the most common of the 'Peak' classes represented, very few 25s now pass through the works except those undergoing stripping before their final call to the breakers yard, the photographs indicate:

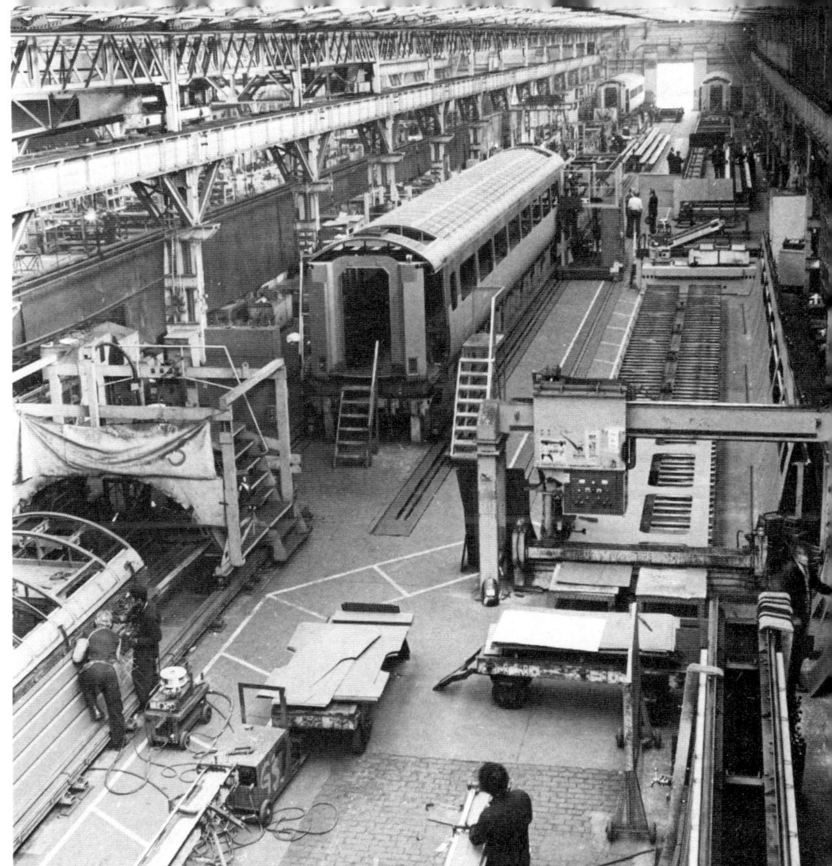

Right and below: Two views within the premises of Derby Litchurch Lane Carriage Works showing the Mk 3 carriage construction line and one of the APT-P driving trailer seconds standing outside the works on temporary bogies awaiting final fitting out before commencing trials.
BREL/John Chalcraft

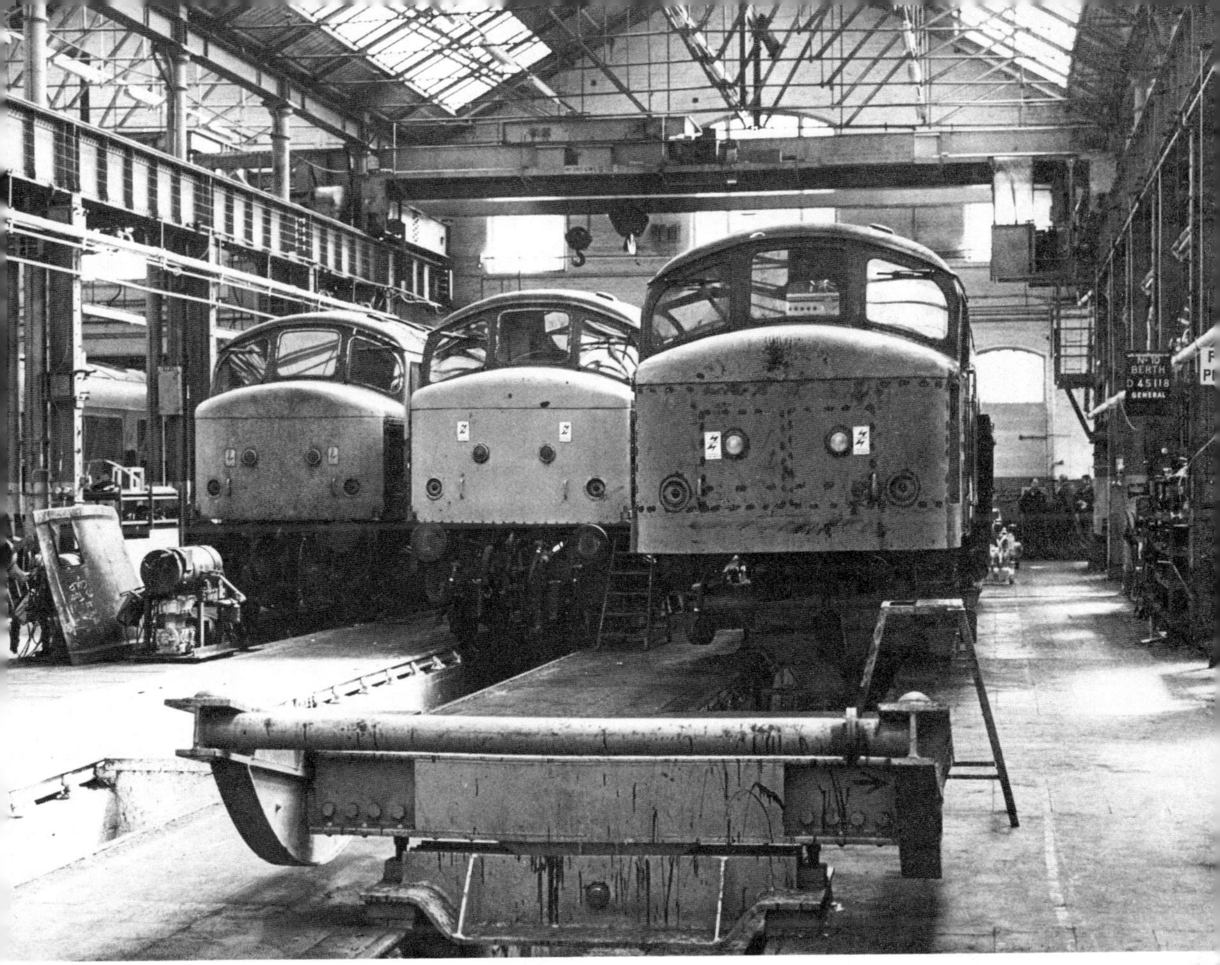

Top left: HST power cars and Classes 45/46 undergoing attention July 1979. *BREL*

Bottom left: HST prototype power car now ADB 975813 and No 45.102 in works. September 1980.

Above: Two ETH 45/1s flank boilered sister loco at Derby (L to R Nos 45.137, 45.020, 45.118) September 1980.

Right: Class 25 No 25.151 undergoes attention with HST power cars. September 1980. *All photographs John Chalcraft*

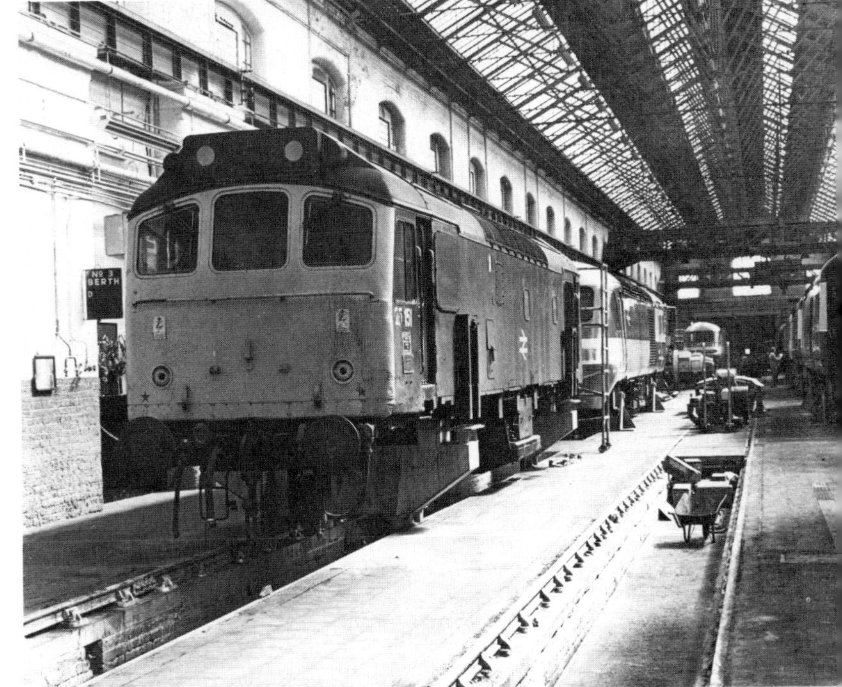

Left: North of Derby the old Ripley branch diverges from the main line at Little Eaton junction, the branch has been truncated so that its present terminus is at Denby Colliery, prime motive power for the branch is the Class 20, in September 1978 Nos 20.043 and 20.005 pass the remains of Denby station with the twice daily freight from Derby. *Roger Kaye*

Centre left: On a fine summer evening in May 1979 Thornaby depot's No. 37.006 heads an unfitted train of flatwagons through pleasant Derbyshire countryside to the north of Duffield. *L. A. Nixon*

Bottom left: Having just passed through Milford tunnel on 26 July 1979 'Peak' No 45.076 heads the 07.30 Swansea-Leeds north past the old goods shed and the remains of the yard at Belper, one of the ventilation shafts for the tunnel is just visible against the background hills. *L. A. Nixon*

Top right: Some 10 miles north of Derby the single track branch line to Matlock (all that remains of the former Midland main line to Manchester) diverges from the main line at Ambergate, normal service on the line is provided by dmus but Adexs to Matlock do bring in some locomotive variety, on 18 March 1978 Railway Pictorial Publications ran the 'Derby Double' railtour from the London area, the final leg of the journey to Matlock being in the hands of a pair of Class 20s, No 20.172 and the prototype for the class now numbered 20.050, the special was photographed as it rejoined the main line at Ambergate junction on the return journey. *L. P. Gater*

Bottom right: On 26 May 1978 an unidentified Class 45 speeds through the Derbyshire Countryside with a northbound (down) express. *L. A. Nixon*

Top left: Clay Cross junction is situated at the point where the NE/SW and the Erewash Valley routes (to Nottingham and Toton) diverge, on a sunny day in September 1979 eth fitted No 47.422 takes the route to Derby with the southbound 10.28 Leeds-Paignton. The old goods shed visible to the right of the junction is used as a workshop by the Crich Tramway museum. *A. R. Kaye*

Bottom left: An interesting flashback to August 1968 shows green liveried 'Peak' No D131 (later 45.074) heading south past the remains of Clay Cross station with an up Leeds-St Pancras express composed of a mixed rake of maroon and blue/grey liveried stock. *J. S. Hancock*

Top: During 1979 Class 56s were introduced on the Barrow Hill (Staveley)-Didcot mgr trains, No 56.025 is seen heading north over the junction with the Erewash Valley line with a return train of empty hoppers, the works of the Clay Cross Co, founded by George Stephenson are visible on the skyline. *Roger Kaye*

Above: An extremely powerful photograph of an unidentified named Class 45 accelerating a northbound express away from Clay Cross junction on 11 December 1976. *L. A. Nixon*

Right: On 8 September 1980 Thornaby depot's No 40.153 heads north down the Midland main line with a train of steel bogie flats specially fitted for the carriage of steel coil. *John Chalcraft*

Left, top and bottom: Between Clay Cross and Chesterfield lies the large coking plant operated by Avenue Carbonisation at Hasland, as one heads north the main works are situated to the left of the line, but, the main exchange sidings with BR are situated to the right of the line with access being made by an overbridge, a considerable amount of local coal traffic is conveyed to the works by rail with trains normally in the hands of Class 20s based for operational purposes at Westhouses depot although maintained at Toton. On 1 June 1979 the unusual combination of Nos 25.070 and 20.153 double-head a lengthy mixed freight past the surprisingly empty exchange sidings, a more normal sight is that of 20s Nos 20.075 and 20.199 heading south past the sidings having disposed of their train of loose fitted coal on 2 October 1980, in the background one of the works shunters shunts wagons before returning to the works environs. *Steve Turner; G. W. Morrison*

Top right: A photograph which typifies the industrial pollution of the area, on a cold and damp February morning the smoke and mist hang heavy over the Avenue Coking plant works as eth fitted No 45.131 heads north with a St Pancras-Sheffield train. *L. A. Nixon*

Centre right: Storm clouds gather over Chesterfield on October 1980 as Class No 47.188 heads a loaded mgr train south, the famous crooked church spire can be glimpsed through the trees, the locomotive is one of the class 47s which although originally fitted with a train heating boiler is now classified as 'NB' the train heat facility having been removed, the hole in the front buffer beam where the steam pipes were once located is easily visible.
G. W. Morrison

Bottom right: As stated elsewhere the Class 44s (original 'Peaks') spent the last decade of their working lives operating from Toton depot on the more menial freight duties, on 16 May 1970 No 8 (later 44.008) still proudly carrying its *Penyghent* nameplates plods past Chesterfield on the freight line which runs round the back of the station buildings with a Toton-Tinsley freight consisting mainly of four wheel mineral wagons. *David Wharton*

Above: BREL works sometimes gain orders for export and upon completion of such orders foreign stock can be found running on the British Rail system for test purposes or en route to its place of transhipment, on 4 August 1980 Class 46 No 46.051 heads a lengthy train of metre gauge stock (on temporary bogies) north past Chesterfield for transhipment to Tanzania via Tyne Dock, the bogies for the coaching stock are mounted on the flatwagons in front of the barrier coach. *Steve Turner*

Left: With the famous twisted church spire of Chesterfield standing on the skyline, Class 40 No 40.058 heads down the freight line past the station with a southbound train of steel coil on 4 September 1980. *Brian Morrison*

Right: To the north of Chesterfield freight and passenger routes diverge, the majority of freight traffic taking the route via Staveley to Tinsley or Rotherham, passenger traffic passes through the heavily industrial area of Sheepbridge before regaining open country, on a sunny July evening in 1979 eth fitted No 47.437 climbs out of Sheepbridge with the 17.05 St Pancras-Sheffield service. *Roger Kaye*

Centre right: On 8 September 1980 workmen stand back from the platform edge at Dronfield as No 45.111 *Grenadier Guardsman* accelerates a down St Pancras-Sheffield train away from a permanent way slack, at the time the station which had been closed for many years was in the process of being rebuilt for re-opening on 5 January 1981. The project being jointly financed by British Rail and the local councils who apparently appreciate the need for direct rail links between the town and Sheffield and Chesterfield particularly during the winter months when road access is sometimes difficult. *John Chalcraft*

Bottom right: To the north of Dronfield the line passes beneath one of the eastern flanks of the Pennine range in Bradway tunnel emerging into the Sheffield suburb of Dore, a short distance from the tunnel mouth a chord line diverges from the main line to join the Hope Valley route to Manchester, very little traffic uses this link, but, one rather unusual working is the Saturday only cement train from Syston (near Leicester) to Earles Sidings near Hope, on 14 February 1981 non-boilered No 47.329 diverges from the main line at Dore South junction with the down train. *Steve Turner*

Top left: Formed from parts of Swindon built 123 and 124 units the 11.25 Hull-Manchester Piccadilly service diverges from the NE/SW main line to take the Hope Valley route at Dore on a dull March afternoon. *John Chalcraft*

Bottom left: The Deltic Class 55 locomotives seldom stray far from the East Coast main line but, on 10 July 1977 the Sheffield Division of British Rail succeeded in securing one of the east coast racehorses in the shape of No 55.007 *Pinza* to head a Sheffield Merrymaker excursion from Chesterfield to Newcastle, Carlisle and Carnforth, the locomotive is pictured passing south through Dore station with the ecs for the outward excursion. *L. A. Nixon*

Top right: An interesting historical photograph for comparison purposes with the preceding illustration showing green liveried Class 47 No 1739 (later 47.146) passing Dore & Totley (later name Dore) station under clear semaphore signals with the York-Poole through train, the date is 1 August 1970. *P. J. Rose*

Bottom right: Yet another grim day for photography on 22 November 1980 finds unusual power for the Sheffield Nunnery Sidings-Manchester Longsight empty vans as Class 31 No 31.106 leaves the city, this working is normally the duty of a Longsight Class 40 and when Class 31s are utilised they normally return light engine immediately from Manchester. *John Chalcraft*

Top left: Somewhat better photographic weather illuminates eth fitted Class 45 No 45.137 on 21 November 1979 as it leaves Sheffield Midland with the 15.00 Sheffield-St Pancras service.
G. W. Morrison

Bottom left: Young enthusiasts enter another number in their books on 4 August 1980 as eth fitted 'Peak' No 45.104 *The Royal Warwickshire Fusiliers* awaits departure from Sheffield Midland with the 13.00 service to St Pancras. *John Chalcraft*

Top right: Sheffield Midland is the originating point for a large number of short and medium range diesel multiple-unit services besides being an important interchange point between local and Inter-City services, on 19 April 1980 units of Classes 108, 110 and 124 stand in the middle roads between platforms awaiting their next turn of duty. *John Chalcraft*

Centre right: Tinsley Depot provides the main source of motive power for the Sheffield area and it is common for smaller powered locomotives to be rostered for summer Saturday and excursion workings originating in the city, on 1 May 1978 No 37.095 finds itself at the head of a Sheffield-Scarborough 'Adex' while No 46.037 stands in an adjacent platform with the 07.30 Birmingham-Newcastle and a 2-car dmu of Class 114 waits its next duty parked in the centre road.
A. O. Wynn

Bottom right: An historic photograph depicting Sheffield Midland station's north end shortly before the replacement of the semaphore signals with colour lights, the date is 11 January 1973. *P. E. Butler*

Left: To the north of Chesterfield lies Tapton junction at the point where the main line into Sheffield diverges from the primarily freight route round the city to Tinsley and Rotherham. On 8 September 1980 having just diverged from the main line No 47.242 heads past Dunston Barlow sidings and signalbox with a northbound engineers' train, No 08.868 is stabled in the sidings between local trip freight working.
John Chalcraft

Centre left: The freight route to Tinsley and Rotherham still boasts a superb selection of semaphore signals operated from small signalboxes situated at strategic points on the line, on 16 April 1978 a Sunday diversion finds a Leeds-Bristol train accelerating past Whittington signalbox and the disused station behind one of the 'Peak' Class 46s No 46.007, the main difference between these locos and the Class 45 being the use of Brush manufactured traction motors in preference to the Crompton-Parkinson variety, unfortunately the apparently early demise of the Class 46 when compared with the '45' would indicate that this choice has not been without its problems. *T. Dodgson*

Bottom left: A large number of heavy block oil trains use the freight route from Tapton junction to Rotherham, on a very cold 26 January 1979 pw staff struggle to clear the heavy snowfall as No 40.091 accelerates a train of oil tanks through Barrow Hill yards. *A. Taylor*

Above: In somewhat better conditions during September 1979, a pair of Class 20s in the form of Nos 20.145 and 20.144 wheel a train of unfitted coal and goods wagons through Staveley, the embankment immediately behind the locos carries the short line to Barrow Hill depot.
L. A. Nixon

Right: Barrow Hill station was closed several years ago but the one remaining platform situated on the down line still sees occasional use, normally when the local diesel depot staff hold their annual open day, on this occasion a regular dmu service is run from Chesterfield. On 5 October 1980 Class 25s Nos 25.038 and 25.073 were used to power an NREA organised excursion and were photographed as they approached the station to pick up passengers for the journey to Doncaster. *Steve Turner*

Left: With the semaphore signal guarding the southbound approach to Staveley in the off position Class 40 No 40.187 approaches Foxlow junction with an engineers' stone train from Mountsorrel (Loughborough) to Healey Mills 12 June 1979. *Roger Kaye*

Below: With the houses of Staveley on the skyline No 31.314 ambles past Foxlow junction with a short train of flatwagons on 5 February 1981. The lines diverging to the left lead to Hall Lane junction and give access to the collieries at Seymour, Markham and Bolsover. *John Chalcraft*

Top right: A signal maintenance man clings precariously to the semaphore signal controlling the up main line towards Staveley on 11 September 1979 as Class 37.168 rumbles past with an up mixed freight conveying predominantly strip steel. *L. A. Nixon*

Bottom right: On 23 May 1978 one of the newly introduced Roumanian-built Class 56s No 56.009 passes the distant signals controlling the approach to Renishaw Park Colliery with a down mgr train from Markham Colliery bound for Rotherwood sidings on the outskirts of Sheffield, at Rotherwood the train will take Class 76 electric power if bound for Fiddlers Ferry power station or the loco will run round to take the Retford line to one of the power stations situated in the East Midlands. *T. Dodgson*

Top: At times when engineering work necessitates the closure of the main line from Sheffield, services are normally routed over the 'Old Road route' out of Sheffield via Nunnery main line junction, Darnall and Woodhouse junction to join the main freight route to Tapton junction at Chesterfield, on a Sunday in March 1979 No 47.457 passes from the Sheffield avoiding line to ex-GC metals at Beighton junction as it runs into the city with the Plymouth-Edinburgh through train. *Roger Kaye*

Above: A civil engineer's cable laying train is a sure sign that the remaining semaphore signals on the Sheffield avoiding line now have a short life expectancy, the northern section of the route into Rotherham having already been converted to colour light. On 5 February 1981. No 47.319 stands on the slow line outside Brookhouse Colliery and Coking plant awaiting orders to proceed. *John Chalcraft*

Above: Besides providing a diversionary route for NE/SW trains the ex-GC route out of Sheffield is also used by local services and some summer Saturday workings to the East Coast, in July 1979 Class 31 No 31.168 finds itself at the head of a Skegness-Sheffield holiday train as it passes through Darnall. Darnall is itself an important part of Sheffield's railway history as it was here that the city's first diesel locomotives were allocated and serviced prior to the opening of Tinsley Yard. *Roger Kaye*

Right: Treeton junction is situated at the point where the line from the east end of Tinsley Yard diverges from the Sheffield avoiding line, in the illustration taken on 23 July 1979 No 31.250 is heading a block steel train from the Rotherham direction past Treeton Junction signalbox, the line diverging to the right leads to Tinsley Yard. *John Chalcraft*

Sheffield-Leeds and York

The northbound exit from Sheffield can hardly be described as scenic, except possibly for the student of industrial archaeology, from the station the line passes into a series of short tunnels and bridges to emerge from beneath the 1,500V dc Woodhead route near the platforms that form Attercliffe Road station, northbound progress is then made between large sheds which form part of the Firth Brown steelmaking complex, passing Sheffield freight terminal on the right, Brightside junction (to Tinsley yard) precedes the vandalised station at Brightside and the local route to Barnsley, Wakefield and Leeds diverges to the left at Wincobank Station junction, before the line passes beneath the northbound M1. Once past the motorway the countryside (?) opens out on the right to provide views of local scrapyards, industrial tips and factories, while on the left small factories and housing cramp the line until Holmes junction and the curve round into Rotherham station are reached. From the motorway bridge onwards the line is parallelled by a freight line that has emerged from the west end of Tinsley yard, this line figures prominently in the projected scheme for Rotherham whereby a link route from Holmes junction onto the freight route will provide access to the proposed Rotherham Central station giving closer proximity to the centre of the town the main routes will be regained at the Aldwarke junction complex.

Rotherham station boasts four platforms although only two of them are in regular use by passengers alighting or joining trains although one of the unused platforms provides access to the booking hall and the town centre, having left Rotherham the line once again parallels the freight route as far as the complex trackwork that forms Aldewarke junction which is situated alongside the BSC Aldwarke works in a maze of industrial and BR owned lines. At Aldwarke junction freight traffic can join the route to the north and passenger traffic can diverge right to take the Doncaster route by means of a large diamond crossing. Since rationalisation of the trackwork in the Wath Road area it is also at this point that the direct routes to York and Leeds diverge to run parallel with each other for some miles before finally diverging from each other at Wath Road junction, the industrial scenery remains unchanged the lines passing a continuous procession of Tar distillers, chemical works etc, just before Wath Road junction the freight route to Wath Yard from Mexborough passes beneath the two lines as the massive Manvers Main Coking plant looms on the horizon (it is uncertain how long this eyesore will remain as in March 1981 it appeared to be out of use and some parts were being demolished).

The York route diverges right at this point to run down the side of the industrial complex and pass through Bolton-on-Dearne station and gain open countryside, the countryside being dotted with the spoil tips and pitheads of the extensive local coal working, after Moorthorpe station the route passes over the Leeds-Doncaster main line then continues north to reach the mining town of Pontefract with its run-down Baghill station, Pontefract also boasts a second station named Monkhill which is situated on the Leeds, Goole/Hull cross-country route which crosses the NE/SW route between Pontefract and Knottingley, spurs from the Leeds-Hull route connect with the NE/SW primarily to enable access for the local MGR trains to reach the large Ferrybridge power station which is situated on the left of the main route. Some two miles further the main line joins the route from Normanton at Burton Salmon junction, the main mining area has now been left behind with the majority of open country being used for agricultural purposes, although the existence of the Selby Drift mine and future mining developments in the Selby area could alter this landscape considerably. At Church Fenton the Leeds-York main line curves in from the left to form a four track section which continues past Ulleskelf where the earthworks for the Selby diversion of the ECML can be seen, to be joined by the East Coast main line at Chaloners Whin junction, the two lines then pass through the sizeable Dringhouses Yard before reaching the splendour of York station with its magnificent overall roof. A large percentage of freight traffic diverges from the passenger lines about a ¼-mile before York station to take the freight line which passes York Carriage Works before rejoining the main at Clifton.

As the York route diverges to the right the main line to Leeds plunges through the heart of the Manvers Coking plant complex emerging into a semi industrial environment which then breaks to give open country, on the left it is possible to see the sizeable yards at Wath, complete with locomotive depot, and, at the present time representatives of the Woodhead routes Class 76s. The line now follows the course of the River Dearne as it curves through Darfield to reach Cudworth and then on to Royston, once again semaphore signalling is in evidence and this remains for the majority of the journey into Leeds via the old Midland route. The line abounds with the remains of old junctions, signs of a bygone

Above: on a bitterly cold January night in 1979 a pair of 'Peaks', eth No 45.136 and steam heated No 46.048 stand at the north end of Sheffield Midland station having just arrived from the south-west. *Peter R. Walton*

era when the use of the railway as a prime mover of transport and public service was recognised, shortly after passing Cudworth we pass Royston, at one time the operating base for a large allocation of freight locomotives, but, nowadays few people would even recognise the remains of the old locomotive depot which have now reverted back to nature. The next feature of note is the Leeds-Doncaster main line which our route passes over at Walton on the outskirts of Wakefield and shortly after Oakenshaw South junction is reached, at this point trains which enter Leeds via Wakefield diverge to the left, the former Midland route carrying straight on to pass Normanton and the splendid semaphores situated at Goose Hill junction, Normanton station is still in use if but a shadow of its former self, but, once again there is little sign of the old shed which was situated to the right after the station before Altofts Junction.

At Altofts junction a further divergence of routes occurs the route to York via Castleford diverging to the right, this route being taken by some of the NE/SW route trains (others use the more direct route via Pontefract already mentioned), the line is joined by the local route from Leeds at Whitwood junction to pass through Castleford, run past the NCB pit at Fryston and finally join the direct route at Burton Salmon junction.

Trains for Leeds diverge left at Altofts junction, to pass the small local station of Altofts, run through Woodlesford and into the Leeds suburbs through Stourton passing the large inland freight development by Garonor (UK) who have realised the importance of good rail connections, and Stourton Freightliner depot which is built on the site of the old Stourton motive power depot, the final miles into Leeds are through the heavily industrialised area of Hunslet, home of the Hunslet Engine Company and the Middleton Railway Trust, the latter still providing a regular freight service for its customers despite being primarily a preservation line running steam trains at weekends, having passed Hunslet the line curves past Leeds Holbeck depot (on the left) where examples of Classes 47, 45, 40 and 31 will probably be present, to pass beneath the line from Doncaster and join the line from Manchester, and Bradford before reaching Leeds City station.

The second route into Leeds which is taken by NE/SW trains diverges from the ex-Midlands main line at Oakenshaw South junction to join ex-L&Y metals at Oakenshaw junction before approaching Wakefield past the power station and the old Wakefield engine shed which is now in use for wagon repair purposes, the line then joins the line from Normanton (Goose Hill junction) just outside Wakefield Kirkgate station, the station being primarily used for local traffic the majority of NE/SW trains take the through route to diverge right at the west end of the station layout, taking the short steeply graded spur from Ings junction to West Riding junction to join the main line from Doncaster and stop in the modernised Wakefield Westgate station. From Wakefield the route passes through the remains of a heavily mined area with associated spoil tips, winding gear etc, to the railway historian there is also much evidence of local lines closed during recent times and the remains of the sizeable Ardley depot can still be seen before the route drops down into the suburbs of Leeds to diverge right from the Bradford line at Gelders Road junction and pass behind Holbeck depot on a series of high walled bridges over the old Midland route from Normanton and into Leeds City station.

Top: Until the closing of the Woodhead route very little freight was diagrammed to pass through Sheffield Midland station, one of the more regular workings was the cement working from Carlisle to Hope Cement works which was routed over the Settle and Carlisle line to Leeds and then via the main line through Sheffield to take the Hope valley route at Dore to the south of Sheffield, on Saturday 19 April 1980 Longsight based No 40.110 emerges from the tunnel and enters the station precincts with this working.
John Chalcraft

Above: In July 1975 an unidentified Class 45 in original condition with split headcode panels climbs away from Sheffield past Attercliffe Road, the train is just emerging from the tunnel beneath the Manchester-Sheffield electrified line and the overhead catenary can be clearly seen behind the locomotive. *L. A. Nixon*

Right: The 09.50 Edinburgh-Plymouth was the normal means for returning ex works Class 50s to the Western region after Doncaster Works overhaul, on 26 September 1980 No 50.003 *Temeraire* approaches Sheffield Midland station past Attercliffe Road station. *Roger Kaye*

Below: One of the non-boilered Class 47/3s No 47.302 ambles past the site of the old Grimethorpe steam shed with a Healey Mills-Earles Sidings (Hope) train of cement empties, the large sheds behind the train were part of one of the Sheffield steel factories and at the time of writing are being demolished, a Class 37 waits in the sidings with a steel train, September 1979. *L. A. Nixon*

Right: Holmes junction lies to the south-west of Rotherham station and used to provide a link between the Sheffield-Leeds line and the Rotherham-Chesterfield line via Barrow Hill, unfortunately like many lines in the area it has since been lifted, the box was replaced when the colour light signalling in the area became operational and has since been raised to the ground, Class 47 No 47.051 passes the box on 24 July 1975 at the head of the 11.45 Cardiff-Newcastle. *Philip D. Hawkins*

RED BULL
40106
Buffet

Left: The Rotherham area has seen considerable change during recent years, the track to the right of the train in the photograph has now been lifted, eliminating the connection from the freight line to the main passenger route to the south of Rotherham Masborough station, the freight only route to Tinsley yard and to Chesterfield can be seen diverging to the right background. The train headed by No 40.111 on 6 March 1978 is also of interest as it is the Cleethorpes-Manchester empty newspapers, this train is sometimes pressed into revenue earning service between Doncaster and Sheffield according to requirements, at Sheffield the '40' will run round the stock removing same to Nunnery Carriage sidings where the stock will be split, the '40' and news vans continuing on their journey to Manchester some two hours later. *T. Dodgson*

Below left: On a bitterly cold 1 December 1978 the green liveried No 40.106 has just passed through Rotherham Masborough as it rounds Holmes curve at the head of the Cleethorpes-Manchester empty news vans. *Roger Kaye*

Right: An enthusiasts' special headed by No 55.022 *Royal Scots Grey* approaches Rotherham Masborough on 21 April 1979 from the freight only Sheffield avoiding line, the colour light signals are obviously operational as the arms have been removed from the semaphores prior to final demolition the box also appears derelict, all operations being handled by the Sheffield panel. *G. W. Morrison*

Centre right: Before the removal of the semaphores, No 37.246 has passed Rotherham Masborough and taken the avoiding line with a southbound block steel train on 25 July 1978. Sadly the superb gantry of semaphore signals has now been demolished. *T. Dodgson*

Bottom right: As most enthusiasts will know the Class 56 locomotives were initially built in Roumania, considerable testing of early class members took place before they entered revenue earning service, on 1 September 1977 the prototype No 56.001 passes through Rotherham Masborough with a test train. *K. Connolly*

Left: On 6 May 1980 No 45.019 curves the 11.45 Cardiff-Newcastle through Rotherham Masborough station. *John Chalcraft*

Centre left: One of the earlier series of Class 31, No 31.111 without the route indicator panel accelerates a short engineers' train through the normally unused eastern side platforms at Rotherham on 6 May 1980. The two platforms furthest away from the passenger exit to the town centre are used for passenger service access being via the covered footbridge. *John Chalcraft*

Bottom left: On a fine September morning in 1977 English Electric Class 37 No 37.141 has an easy task as it ambles past Rotherham Masborough North Junction signalbox with two brakevans. *G. W. Morrison*

Top right: Another piece of Britain's railway heritage disappears on 6 March 1978 as an old LMS signal gantry is removed from its site just north of Rotherham Masborough station, a Class 31 attends as a 4-car train composed of two 2-car sets passes on a Sheffield-York service. *T. Dodgson*

Bottom right: Freight for the north which does not leave Tinsley Yard via Treeton junction can also leave via Shepcote Lane and Tinsley station junctions to gain the freight only route which runs parallel with the passenger route through Rotherham, it is on this route that it is proposed that BR build the projected Rotherham Central station giving a closer proximity to the centre of the town, access to the route would be via a curve to be built from Holmes junction, on 24 July 1975 Class 31 No 31.124 heads a class 8 freight through Rotherham Road yards towards Doncaster. *Philip D. Hawkins*

8D32

Left: Wath Road junction is situated some six miles north of Rotherham at the point where the direct route to York and the route to Leeds diverge, the area immediately to the north of the junction is heavily industrialised and the main line to Leeds passes through the heart of the industrial complex, with the light of a dull summer afternoon already failing and the industrial gloom of the Manvers Main coking plant making the situation worse No 45.052 heads south past the signalbox on 13 August 1980 with the 14.32 Leeds-Plymouth. *John Chalcraft*

Centre left: Some six months later on the 4 February 1981 No 47.082 *Atlas* swings the 07.00 Newcastle-Bristol round the curve from the direct route to York (via Pontefract) and heads south past Wath Road, in a period of six months the junction layout has been completely remodelled, the four track route from Leeds having been reduced to two tracks and the semaphore signals have been replaced by colour light signalling although the now out of use box remains. *John Chalcraft*

Bottom left: Trains to Leeds take one of two routes to the city after passing Wath Road, the lines diverging at Crofton West junction, one route being the old Midland via Normanton the other route is via Wakefield Kirkgate and Westgate, normally with a stop at Westgate the latter route uses ex-L&Y metals and passes the old Wakefield motive power depot which is now used for wagon repair purposes, a large amount of traffic in the area is generated by coal for use at the large power stations at Drax, Eggborough and Ferrybridge, on 7 July 1976 No 47.371 prepares to run round its train of mgr wagons outside the old depot before heading its train to Eggborough, the majority of these workings have now been taken over by Class 56s based at Knottingley depot. *G. W. Morrison*

bove: The ex-L&Y route out of Vakefield is also used for diversions of .eeds-Kings Cross trains when need rises the trains are normally routed via ‹nottingley regaining the ECML at haftholme Junction just north of)oncaster, on Sunday 8 July 1979 the 6.15 Bradford-Kings Cross heads out of Vakefield past the old mpd in the apable hands of 'Deltic' No 55.010. *. W. Morrison*

entre right: With the cooling towers of Vakefield power station in the ackground No 37.103 rounds the curve nto Wakefield Kirkgate on 5 February 981 with a Loughborough-Healey Mills ngineers' train. *A. O. Wynn*

ottom right: The 10.28 Leeds to aignton is one of the NE/SW route ains that take the circuitous route via Vakefield with a stop at Wakefield Vestgate, on 5 February 1981 No 47.402 eads the train across the junction at ne east end of Kirkgate station, in the ackground a Class 40 approaches on ne line from Goose Hill junction, lormanton. *A. O. Wynn*

Above: A view from Wakefield Kirkgate as 'Peak' No 46.048 heads the Leeds portion of the 08.15 from Plymouth pas Wakefield West Junction box to take th short spur to Wakefield Westgate, the main line from London crosses the bridge in the background and the line diverging to the left runs out to Horbury junction and Healey Mills Yard.
A. O. Wynn

Left: On the other route into Leeds via Normanton semaphore signals still abound until the Leeds suburbs are reached although at the start of 1981 obvious signs of cable laying for colour lights were visible at a number of places, on 4 February 1981 eth fitted 'Peak' No 45.112 approaches a fine upper quadrant signal near Normanton, the train is the 07.40 Cardiff-Newcastle, it will diverge from the main line at Altofts Junction to the north of Normanton and travel through Castleford to regain the main route to York at Burton Salmon. *John Chalcraf*

Right: Goose Hill junction lies to the south of Normanton at a point where the line to Wakefield diverges from the ex Midland route (in the background). On 4 February 1981 a pair of Class 25s Nos 25.150 and 25.152 head an engineers' train for Healey Mills towards Wakefield. *John Chalcraft*

Centre right: With the semaphore signal at clear Bescot depot's Class 47 No 47.298 accelerates the 16.39 Leeds-Bristol away from Goose Hill junction, Normanton on 13 September 1979. This train was one of the first NE/SW expresses rostered for HST sets from 5 October 1981. *G. W. Morrison*

Below: On 13 September 1979 one of the Western Region's named, boilered Class 47s No 47.080 *Titan* nears its destination as it passes the remains of Normanton station with the 09.58 Weymouth-Leeds. *G. W. Morrison*

Above: Despite their reluctance to allocate the Class 55 'Deltics' to enthusiast specials when requested British Rail apparently has no qualms i using the locomotives upon their own 'Merrymaker' excursions for enthusiast clientele, on the 23 July 1978, No 55.00 *Meld* approaches Leeds past Stourton a the head of a special to Carlise, sadly the locomotive was the third member o the class to be withdrawn in 1980. *G. W. Morrison*

Centre left: More normal power in the Leeds area is the heavyweight Class 40, one of the later members of the class with central indicator panels, No 40.192 approaches the city past Stourton Freightliner depot, in the background behind the fourth van a Park Royal 2-ca dmu now in departmental service stands in the sidings. *Steve Turner*

Bottom left: During early summer the British Rail/Fisons weedkilling trains visit the majority of the British Rail system, Monday 14 May 1979 finds the train approaching the Hunslet area of Leeds on the old Midland main line behind No 40.009. *G. W. Morrison*

bove: One of the classes apparently
lestined for an early demise during the
ecession of the late 1970s early 1980s is
he Class 46 version of the 'Peak',
lthough outwardly the same as
nembers of Class 45, these locomotives
re slightly heavier and have different
raction motors. On 10 May 1980 No
6.029 passes the siding leading to the
vorks of the Hunslet Engine Company
s it leaves Leeds with the 16.38
eeds-Bristol. *G. W. Morrison*

ight: Shortly after leaving Leeds City
tation trains via the old Midland Route
o the south swing beneath the main
Eastern Region) route to London and
urve past Leeds Holbeck motive power
epot, on 10 October 1980 Class 40 No
0.091 has just traversed the Settle and
arlisle line and heads south with the
6.00 Carlisle-Earles Sidings (Hope
alley) cement empties. *Steve Turner*

Left: One of the Leeds City centre office blocks towers over Class 45 No 45.011 as it approaches its destination on 20 September 1975 at the head of the 10.30 Paignton-Leeds, a Class 31 waits the road to Leeds Holbeck depot.
Brian Morrison

Below: An impressive panoramic photograph of the Leeds City approaches as eth 'Peak' No 45.106 approaches the station at the head of a Paignton-Leeds working, in the background one of the local shunters is having considerable difficulty in moving a lengthy rake of parcels stock, the 2 car diesel multiple-units in the foreground are forming the next service on the route to Sheffield via Barnsley.
Brian Morrison

ight: On a damp March afternoon in 981 one of the Western Region's amed Class 47s No 47.511 *Thames* eads the 09.50 Edinburgh-Plymouth ut of Castleford through the reverse urves at Castleford Gates. *Roger Kaye*

elow: Certain trains for York and ewcastle do not travel via the direct oute from Sheffield to York via ontefract but take the ex Midland route s far as Normanton, where they iverge to take the route through astleford to gain the main line at urton Salmon, in May 1974 an nidentified Class 40 swings a freight om Healey Mills across the junction vith the spur off the Leeds-Knottingley ne and enters the run down and andalised Castleford Station. . *G. Glover*

Left: Castleford as many readers know lies in the middle of the Yorkshire coalfield and collieries and pitheads are a common sight to the seasoned rail traveller, on an unknown date in April 1974 NCB personnel are having difficulty re-railing their yard shunter as a Class 37 (unidentified) heads a rake of 100tonne oil tank wagons past Fryston Colliery. *J. G. Glover*

Below: Mining subsidence is a common occurrence in areas of extensive underground coal working and pw slacks abound on the railway lines in the Pontefract area, Class 40 No 40.156 heads a short mixed freight past the site of a particularly bad subsidence as it heads for Burton Salmon on 2 March 1974 with a short mixed freight bound for York, (the pithead on the skyline is that of Fryston). *M. Mitchell*

Right: With the gigantic cooling towers of the CEGB generating station at Ferrybridge as a backdrop a 3-car Metro-Cammell dmu heads north on the direct Sheffield-York route via Pontefract Baghill during April 1979. *L. A. Nixon*

Centre right: Summer Saturdays often cause British Rail to turn out low powered locomotives for longer distance workings, although their use during the week is somewhat rarer, on Thursday 11 September 1979 Class 31 No 31.203 finds itself at the head of a relief working to the 09.50 Birmingham-Newcastle, the train is passing Burton Salmon junction having travelled from Sheffield via Normanton. *G. W. Morrison*

Below: The huge power stations in the Knottingley area consume more coal than local pits can provide and considerable tonnages are moved by rail from the County Durham coalfield, these trains normally change engines in Clifton yards at York. On 4 September 1979 No 47.179 approaches Burton Salmon from York with a southbound mgr working, the majority of these workings are now handled by Class 56s recently based at Knottingley. *G. W. Morrison*

790

Left: Steam locos from the National Railway Museum at York are frequently loaned out to preservation centres or used on 'circular railtours' from York to York via Harrogate on such an occasion they pass through the large station situated at Church Fenton, on 14 July 1977 ex-LNWR 'Precedent' class No 790 *Hardwicke* and the Duke of Sutherland's coach stand at Church Fenton station. *G. W. Morrison*

Bottom left: The more common view of Church Fenton taken on 6 December 1980 as 'Peak' No 45.036 heads the lengthy Newcastle-Redbank (Manchester) parcels through the station, in the distance the direct Sheffield route diverges to the right. *John Chalcraft*

Top right: The last steam loco to be built by BR, Standard '9F' No 92220 *Evening Star* hauls ex-GNR Atlantic *Henry Oakley* out of York past Copmanthorpe en route to the Keighley & Worth Valley Railway on 20 May 1977. *G. W. Morrison*

Centre right: On 10 May 1980 one of Thornaby depot's Class 37s No 37.001 heads for Leeds as it leaves York and Chaloners Whin junction with an oddly assorted train consisting of a rake of freight-liner wagons and an apparently unfitted selection of flatwagons hence the brake van. *G. W. Morrison*

Bottom right: At times of heavy traffic servicing of excursion and other stock which cannot be handled at York is sometimes handled at Leeds Neville Hill, on 7 April 1979 No 40.015 *(Aquitania)* approaches York past the junction with the East Coast route at Chaloners Whin junction. *Steve Turner*

Left: In pre HST days when the 'Deltics' were prime motive power for the East Coast route Finsbury Park depot's No 55.012 *Crepello* accelerates past Dringhouses yard as it leaves York with the 08.00 Edinburgh-Kings Cross, 13 September 1977. *G. W. Morrison*

Centre left: 'Peak' class locomotives are by no means common on mgr workings, but, on 14 August 1980 No 46.050 finds itself entrusted with a southbound coal train as it heads south past Dringhouses Yard, the yard is obviously suffering from the early effects of the economic recession. *Steve Turner*

Bottom left: York possesses a very important through route which bypasses the main station area, this route leaves the main line at Holgate Junction just south of York station and rejoins the main line at Clifton to the north, in the summer of 1979 No 40.032 *(Empress of Canada)* arcs its way off the freight route past Holgate junction as it heads a mixed freight south to Dringhouses Yard. *Barry J. Nicolle*

Top right: York Minster provides an impressive backdrop as 'Deltic' No 55.014 leaves York station with the 15.50 York-Kings Cross semi-fast in July 1980. *John Chalcraft*

Bottom right: English Electric Types 4 and 5 at York on 18 April 1980 as No 55.018 arrives at the station with the 09.50 from Edinburgh to Plymouth, Class 50 No 50.007 *Hercules* prepares to take over the working for the second part of its journey to the south-west, the Class 50 had arrived at York after powering the 19.34 Bristol-Newcastle the previous night. *Roger Kaye*

Left: A very early 1970s photograph of York station as green liveried No D6778 (now 37.078) accelerates through the centre road with a southbound train of vanfits. *David Wharton*

Below: A final look at York with one of the magnificent 'Deltic' Class 55s that for so long had made the East Coast route their own as No 55.003 *Meld* complete with the white window treatment applied by Finsbury Park Depot excites the watching enthusiasts after its arrival beneath York's famous 'over-all' roof with the 14.05 semi-fast from Kings Cross, on 26 January 1980, sadly the locomotive was the third casualty in the Class 55 withdrawal programme being taken out of service after a major failure and condemned on 5 January 1981. *John Chalcraft*

HST Introduction

Monday 5 October 1981 will be noted as a date of some importance to many people linked with both rail operations and travel upon the North East/South West axis with the introduction of the first cross-country HST services linking Bristol and Plymouth with Leeds, the first trains to be diagrammed for HSTs being the 07.00 Bristol and the 08.20 Plymouth services to Leeds with the 14.37 and 16.38 return services. The enthusiast will mourn the passing of both trains, particularly the 07.00 which regularly produced small locomotives for power, with the subsequent possibility of banking assistance up the Lickey incline, but, besides the improvement in comfort the 07.00 in its new form can now boast a buffet car, indeed a welcome addition for the benefit of the early morning traveller. The Plymouth-Edinburgh and return service was diagrammed for HST from 2 November, and other services will follow as more units become available, although loco haulage will remain from the South West on trains to Manchester and Liverpool.

One noticeable difference between the first and second generation Class 253 units is the replacement of one of the trailer first coaches by an additional trailer second, although one must question the suitability of rigid formations when confronted with the possible loadings of 750-800 people that are not unknown on certain Sunday evening trains on the route.

Below: On the first day of the revised service (5 October 1981) the inaugural IC125 service arrives at Derby with the 07.00 ex-Bristol to be met by local press and officialdom. *A. O. Wynn*

Above: The second northbound HST service on 5 October forming the 08.20 Plymouth-Leeds accelerates away from Burton-on-Trent, the revised train formation of five trailer seconds, buffet, and the single trailer first being clearly visible. *A. O. Wynn*

Left: The 07.00 Bristol-Leeds train seen leaving Birmingham New Street station on 27 October 1981. *John Chalcraft*

Below left: The first generation '253' units have been associated with the Western Region for some years, but, apart from running to and from Derby for attention have never made regular incursions onto NE/SW metals although skirting the route at both Bristol and occasionally Gloucester. No 253 020 makes a smoky exist as it leaves Bristol on 6 May 1959 with the 15.25 service to Paddington, the two trailer firsts are clearly visible at the front of the train. *John Chalcraft*

100

THINGS TO DO IN

NEBRASKA

BEFORE YOU

DIE

Orpheum
Omaha Performing Arts Presents
MILLION DOLLAR QUARTET
Feb 18-23
watchfire

100 THINGS TO DO IN NEBRASKA BEFORE YOU DIE

TIM AND LISA TRUDELL

Reedy Press
PO Box 5131
St. Louis, MO 63139, USA
www.reedypress.com

Library of Congress Control Number: 2019952604

ISBN: 9781681062488

Design by Jill Halpin

All photos provided by the author unless otherwise noted.

Printed in the United States of America
20 21 22 23 24   5 4 3 2 1

Please note that websites, phone numbers, addresses, and company names are subject to change or cancellation. We did our best to relay the most accurate information available, but due to circumstances beyond our control, please do not hold us liable for misinformation. When exploring new destinations, please do your homework before you go.